WEEKEND
WEALTH TRANSFER

WEEKEND
WEALTH TRANSFER

How Black Churches Move
Billions of Dollars out of
Black Communities and
How to Move It Back

Gwen Richardson

FIRST EDITION

Cover design by Cory Wright

ISBN: 978-1539373643
ISBN-10:   1539373649

10 9 8 7 6 5 4 3 2 1

Printed in the United States of America

To future generations of African-American children

TABLE OF CONTENTS

INTRODUCTION 1

CHAPTER 1: HISTORICAL SIGNIFICANCE OF THE BLACK CHURCH 6

CHAPTER 2: SHOULD BLACK CHURCHES MAKE A CONSCIOUS EFFORT TO SUPPORT BLACK BUSINESSES? 13

CHAPTER 3: ANNUAL COLLECTIVE INCOME OF BLACK CHURCHES 19

CHAPTER 4: WEALTH TRANSFER BEGINS ON MONDAY MORNING 29

CHAPTER 5: MORTGAGES, INTEREST PAYMENTS, LEASES, UTILITIES AND OTHER COMMON CHURCH EXPENDITURES 47

CHAPTER 6: IT'S EASIER SAID THAN DONE 56

CHAPTER 7: WHAT CHURCHES CAN DO 81

CHAPTER 8: WHAT PARISHIONERS CAN DO 96

CHAPTER 9: WHAT ENTREPRENEURS CAN DO....116

CHAPTER 10: WHAT THE FUTURE COULD LOOK LIKE 123

ACKNOWLEDGEMENTS 129

INTRODUCTION

Every Sunday in black churches across America collection plates are passed and parishioners insert their tithes and offerings. The very next day, as those funds are deposited in church bank accounts, the transfer of millions of dollars occurs as those funds are placed in financial institutions that are not owned by African Americans. However, the weekend's wealth transfer does not end there. It continues throughout the remainder of the week as the majority of mortgage companies, landlords, insurance companies, and vendors most black churches utilize are also not African American-owned. This wealth transfer occurs largely unconsciously but its impact is enormous.

Exact figures on the cumulative number of dollars raised annually by black churches are hard to come by. However, based on available data, estimates range from $6 billion to $25 billion per year. The bulk of these funds come directly from the incomes of African-American parishioners who donate to the church, and the church then transfers those funds to institutions and businesses owned by other ethnic

1

groups through a variety of ways that will be detailed in this book.

This wealth transfer is a relatively recent phenomenon and did not occur prior to the 1960s when black churches were small and localized, essentially operating in local communities with limited budgets. Several demographic and societal shifts triggered this new reality, including the explosion of the black middle class that occurred after the civil rights movement and the resultant migration out of the inner cities to the suburbs following social integration.

There is a widely held belief that a dollar circulates only six hours in the black community; however, verifying this statement is challenging. Data to substantiate it is nearly impossible to find and is most often attributed to the NAACP and the Selig Center for Economic Growth at the University of Georgia.[1] Some even consider the six-hour figure to be an urban legend. Yet if we examine the flow of money via the black church, the wealth transfer seems to occur within 24 hours.

The transfer would not be so problematic if a reciprocating money stream was flowing from other communities into black-owned enterprises. In other words, if churches from other ethnic groups were collecting funds each weekend and transferring them to black-owned banks and businesses, the two realities would be balanced, with essentially one cancelling out the other. Instead, all of the funds are moving in one direction—away from black communities and entrepreneurs. This is analogous to a farmer pouring gallons of water into a bucket with tubing connected to another farmer's irrigation system. As soon as the water is poured into the bucket, it quickly leaks out of the bottom and the farmer loses all the water needed to irrigate his own land.

Another reason this weekend wealth transfer is so problematic is that it compounds the already rapid flight of dollars out of black communities. Only 2 percent of black consumer dollars are spent in the black community, according to Teri Williams, president and COO of OneUnited, America's largest black-owned bank. "If that 2 percent that stayed in the community moved to 10 percent, we could create a million jobs in our community. That's how significant this is," said Williams in a July 15, 2016, interview with *MadameNoire*, an online lifestyle publication for African-American women.[2] One or two small shifts in how black churches direct their expenditures could make an enormous difference.

Individuals from other ethnic groups may perceive any effort at wealth retention to be racism at its worst. "The race of the church, the parishioners, and where the money ultimately goes should not be an issue within the body of Christ," some might say. The problem with that approach is that it completely ignores the drain of resources—the divestment—away from communities where the majority of residents are African American.

Actions that are considered routine within predominantly white churches—doing business with companies where the owner is also white—may appear to be simply a coincidence. But the devastating impact of black churches not doing likewise within our own communities affects the infrastructure, education and employment prospects of millions of black people in multiple generations. To ignore the pain and suffering of so many as a consequence is, in a word, unChristian. While virtually every other group in America practices group economics, would non-black Christians prefer that African Americans operate with both hands tied behind our backs?

Some may incorrectly perceive this book to be an attack on the black church, but that is not its purpose. As a preacher's kid and a committed Christian, I am well aware of the centuries-long institutional importance of the black church. In actuality, in many ways leaders within black churches have limited options for simultaneously retaining this wealth among African Americans and maintaining sound stewardship over church coffers. Most of the wealth transfer occurs because black pastors simply have no choice.

This book is my second installment in a series on group economics, the missing link and Achilles heel of African-American economic progress. The first installment, *Why African Americans Can't Get Ahead: And How We Can Solve It With Group Economics*, was published in 2008. The purpose of this book is to explore the economic impact of the transfer of wealth away from black communities via the black church, its impact on those communities, and strategies to reverse this trend.

CHAPTER 1

HISTORICAL SIGNIFICANCE OF THE BLACK CHURCH

There is no doubt that the black church is a pivotal institution among African Americans. Throughout United States history the black church has been a vital vehicle for social and political progress. During both the abolitionist and civil rights movements, the church was the central meeting place for developing plans and strategies and was also a safe haven for those seeking refuge from racial animus. Before the Civil War, some black churches were utilized as stops on the Underground Railroad.

For example, the first African Methodist Episcopal (AME) church in Indianapolis, Indiana, Bethel AME Church, became active in the anti-slavery movement, often harboring fugitive slaves en route to Canada. The congregation of Bethel AME Zion Church of Reading, Pennsylvania, was active in the Underground Railroad during the years leading up to the Civil War. And the Second Baptist Church of Detroit, Michigan, established in 1836 when 13 former slaves decided to leave the First Baptist Church because of its discriminatory practices, was also a stop on the Underground Railroad.[3]

"The black church community is the only black institution that successfully survived centuries of slavery, Jim Crow semi-slavery, and government-directed benign neglect," writes Dr. Claud Anderson in his book, *PowerNomics: The National Plan to Empower Black America*.[4] The church is to the black community as the heart is to a human being, and its importance as a vital institution cannot be overstated.

Moreover, as a group, African Americans are markedly more religious on a variety of measures than the U.S. population as a whole, according to a survey conducted by the Pew Research Center's Forum on Religion and Public Life. In its 2014 U.S. Religious Landscape Study, the Pew Research Center found that fully 87 percent of African Americans describe themselves as belonging to one religious group or another. Eighty-three percent of blacks express an unequivocal belief in God, 79 percent say religion is very important in their lives (compared with 56 percent among all U.S. adults), 47 percent attend religious services at least once per week, and 73 percent pray on a daily basis.[5]

In addition, the vast majority of African Americans are Protestant (78 percent). In fact, African Americans stand out as the most Protestant racial and ethnic group in the U.S.[6]

These strongly held religious beliefs translate into stable church membership rolls among America's black churches. Indeed, while Christians are losing their share of the overall U.S. population, the Pew Research Center survey reveals that black denominations are bucking that trend, holding to a steady membership base.[7] Of particular significance is the fact that the share of African-American millennials who affiliate with historically black churches is similar to that of older churchgoers.[8]

Black Churches Not Immune To Economic Downturns

The central role that the black church plays within black communities does not inoculate it from the effects of economic downturns. Triggered by the 2008 financial crisis which resulted in the foreclosures of more than six million homes, a surge in church foreclosures also occurred.[9] Of the 654 religious congregations to file for Chapter 11 bankruptcy protection between 2006 and 2013, 60 percent had black pastors or predominantly black membership, according to a published paper by Pamela Foohey, an associate professor at the Indiana University Maurer School of Law. Black churches have been disproportionately affected considering they make up only 21 percent of U.S. congregations, according to a 2012 analysis.[10]

"Churches are among the final institutions to get foreclosed upon because banks have not wanted to look like they are being heavy handed with the churches," said Scott Rolfs, managing director of Religious and Education finance at the investment bank Ziegler in an interview with the Reuters news organization.[11]

The negative impact on black churches during times of economic crises is all too familiar to Rev. Dean Rodgers, senior pastor of the Salvation and Praise Worship Center (www.salvationandpraise.org) in Hampton, Va. "During the crash of 2008, a lot of churches lost their buildings," says Rodgers, whose church has about 80 members. "A lot of pastors jumped out there and bought large buildings when the economy boomed," he added, "but they started having serious financial challenges around 2009."

A case in point is Carter Tabernacle Christian Methodist Episcopal Church, Orlando's oldest black church, which filed for Chapter 11 bankruptcy in September 2016 even as it marked its 100th anniversary. According to court records, the church's financial issues were tied to a mortgage for $3.5 million originated in 2001, when the housing economy was booming.[12]

Largely due to the size of his congregation, Rodgers has always retained full-time employment elsewhere so that his church, which he started in 1994, can avoid the expense of paying him a full-time salary. "I've always worked a full-time job outside of the church," says Rodgers, "and during economic downturns, I have taken a salary cut when finances are short. This lessens the impact on our church's budget when the economy fluctuates."

The most important factor in the increase in church foreclosures lies with the primary source of church revenues—donations by members of the congregation. During the real estate boom, many churches took out additional loans to refurbish or expand their property. After the financial crash, many churchgoers lost their jobs or had their number of work hours reduced. As a result, church donations plunged, and church property values often fell as well.[13] Following foreclosures, churches are either auctioned off or sold to other churches.

Black Church Uniquely Positioned to Facilitate Wealth Transfer

Since the black church plays such a vital role in African-American life, its role in the economic vitality of black communities is essential. Its position as an influential institution provides a unique vehicle to facilitate economic shifts and the transfer of wealth. "Black churches," says Dr. Claud Anderson, "have the potential power to stop the capital drain from the black communities."[14]

In fact, it is unlikely that the concept of wealth transfer can be addressed or be successful *without* the direct involvement of the black church. Examine all of the great movements in the United States that contributed to freedom for African Americans, all of which included an economic component:

- The abolition of slavery;
- The creation of the U.S. network of historically black colleges and universities (HBCUs); and
- The civil rights movement.

Every sweeping political, social, and economic movement that has effected change for African Americans in the history of our nation has occurred with the assistance and full participation of the black church. The movement toward wealth transfer and group economics will not be an exception.

The primary reason is that the black church is the only independent vehicle for information dissemination within the black community. While there are some black-owned media outlets—Radio One and TV One for example—these are used largely for the purposes of entertainment, not information dissemination. None of these entities has viable, in-depth news programming. Even *The Tom Joyner Morning Show*, a nationally-syndicated radio program that reaches millions of African Americans daily, is primarily a vehicle for entertainment.

These outlets are also not independent in that they derive the majority of their revenues from advertising dollars from non-black corporations, which may not look favorably upon efforts to educate the masses with an ideology of economic independence. This forces these outlets toward white-washed content (pun intended).

Thus, the black church is the largest institution through which wealth is transferred out and through which this trend can start to be reversed. It is also an institution that, by and large, African Americans respect and trust to act in their own interests.

CHAPTER 2

SHOULD BLACK CHURCHES MAKE A CONSCIOUS EFFORT TO SUPPORT BLACK BUSINESSES?

Some may question the premise of this book in terms of its focus on the church's role in group economics. In other words, should the black church be involved in group economics or should its focus be strictly on man's spiritual matters, i.e., salvation (repentance, avoidance of sin, and life after death), sacraments (baptism and Holy Communion), and Scripture (teach from the Bible)?

In actuality, the concept of group economics is scripturally sound for a variety of reasons. First, in the early Christian church, offerings were collected for the specific purpose of taking care of the immediate needs of the church, as well as for those within the church body who were in need. In other words, the funds were circulated locally among the parishioners and the local community.

Second, Jesus was not detached from economic matters during his years on Earth. When Peter had been fishing all night and did not catch anything, Jesus offered Peter a way to increase his business, telling him to let down his nets "for a draught" or a catch. Peter then caught so many fish that his

13

nets broke. (Luke 5:1-10). In addition, when Peter indicated to Jesus that taxes (or a tribute) were due to the government, Jesus instructed him to go to the sea, cast down a net, and catch a fish with a coin in its mouth to pay the taxes. (Matthew 17:24).

Third, according to Scripture, a man who does not take care of his family is worse than an unbeliever. "Anyone who does not provide for their relatives, and especially for their own household, has denied the faith and is worse than an unbeliever." (1 Timothy 5:8-NIV) In a similar fashion, the pastor is the leader of his spiritual household—the church body—and should take care of those within its ranks as well as within the surrounding community. The practices of wealth retention and group economics ensure that this occurs.

Fourth, according to Pastor Sammie Holloway of the Breath of Life Christian Center in Memphis, Tenn., prophecy in the Old Testament teaches that Christ would restore the nation of Israel to military and economic power, along with all that is associated with such restoration. "The Bible says that the wealth of the wicked is laid up for the righteous (Proverbs 13:22)," asserts Holloway. Since individuals of other ethnicities are practicing the principle of commercial occupation, Holloway says the focus should be on the group that is not practicing it—in other words, African Americans and other descendants of the biblical character called Ham.

"All over the world, blacks, for the most part, are living at the bottom of the economic chart," says Holloway. "Statistically, we come last when it comes to practicing commerce vertically, as well as horizontally. This, in my opinion, is directly related to our not working the principle found in the scripture." More details about Holloway and his approach to group economics will be discussed in Chapter 6.

Fifth, since churches collect and dispense large sums of money on a regular basis, they, too, should be mindful of how the funds are spent and should strategically spend the funds so that other believers who own businesses can grow and become stronger. Black churches must be aware of the long-term effects of transferring over 90 percent of funds collected to businesses owned by individuals of other ethnicities.

Finally, as stated in Chapter 1, if one uses history as a guide, it is doubtful that the principles of group economics can be taught and reinforced without direct involvement of the black church. The movement toward group economics will not be an exception.

It Depends on the Pastors

Since billions of dollars are donated to black churches by their parishioners annually, one might believe it is a foregone conclusion that black churches make a conscious effort to support black businesses. But this depends on the pastor's commitment to circulating dollars within the black community. If the pastor views this as an important objective, it is more likely to occur. If not, the odds of practicing group economics are not favorable.

Prior to Rev. Kevin Wayne Johnson's tenure at Accokeek First Church of God (www.accokeekchog.org), the previous pastors did not emphasize utilizing black vendors for the services the church needed. When Johnson took over, he made it a priority. "All of my experiences with black-owned vendors have been positive," he says. "The vendors have good quality products and deliver on time."

It will take many hundreds of black pastors to understand this vision and get a revelation regarding the importance of this to the future of black people for it to take root. But every movement starts with a small group of people and grows from there. The doctrine of group economics presented by a pastor, a person of authority that African Americans respect, will have a profound impact on the hearts and minds of the people. However, the pastor would need to possess a genuine understanding and passion about the importance of wealth retention for the effort to succeed.

A previous lack of emphasis on wealth retention may in part be due to the nature of the training that pastors receive. Many black pastors have little more than a high school education, and most of those who do have college degrees studied ministry, religion or humanities. Few have backgrounds in business or economics.

Based on interviews with pastors of churches from around the country, both large and small, the efforts to support black-owned businesses are not seamless and are often challenging.

In general, pastors are permitted to make some unilateral purchasing decisions up to a certain dollar amount, and the threshold varies from church to church. Above the threshold, the deacon board, trustee board, or finance committee will most likely weigh in on the decision.

Pastors are sometimes caught between the desire to support black enterprises and the requirement to provide sound stewardship over church finances. At smaller churches where budgets are limited, price considerations tend to be paramount.

Rev. Henry Prosper says that with a church membership of slightly over 100 members, Westfield must "purchase the highest quality possible for the lowest possible price." The church usually takes bids from three potential vendors and accepts the lowest of the three as long as the services are comparable.

"Unfortunately, black-owned companies will often have the highest price with limited options, so we are unable to do business with them," says Prosper. "But supporting these businesses is something that we would like to do. We simply do not have that many opportunities."

For the Progressive National Baptist Convention (www.pnbc.org), supporting African-American enterprises is part of its mission. "Our convention is the denominational home of Dr. Martin Luther King Jr.," says Dr. Timothy Boddie, general secretary and chief operating officer. "It was founded in 1961, in part, to provide a platform for King and the civil rights movement. Our mission is to wed spirituality with social justice, and as a result, we make an intentional effort to support African-American-owned businesses and encourage our churches to do the same."

Before accepting the position as general secretary in September 2015, Boddie, who holds a doctorate in educational ministry, had pastored two churches, one in Atlanta, Ga., and another in Robersonville, N.C., and also held faculty positions at three historically black colleges— Morehouse, Hampton University, and Shaw University. Supporting black business has been one of his objectives throughout his career.

The black church is the largest institution within the black community that collects and transfers wealth on a regular basis. Whether churches believe they should be involved in group economics or not, they are positioned at the nexus of this generation's quest for economic independence.

CHAPTER 3

ESTIMATING THE ANNUAL COLLECTIVE INCOME OF BLACK CHURCHES

Black buying power is about $1.1 trillion, according to Nielsen consumer reports.[15] This collective amount grows at an extraordinary rate and is expected to be $1.4 trillion by 2020.[16] But the total amount raised by black churches annually through contributions from parishioners and other sources of income is not easy to quantify.

Although much of the American population is familiar with the megachurch phenomenon due to their size and visibility, these large churches are much more an aberration than they are the norm. The millions of dollars raised annually by black megachurches is not representative of the thousands of small churches, most of which have fewer than 100 members. Black churches vary widely in congregation size—from storefront churches with a handful of members to megachurches with tens of thousands of members. But estimates can be derived based on relevant research and calculating percentages of the total annual income of African Americans.

One way of estimating the cumulative funds received by black churches per year is to start with the estimated total income of all African Americans within the United States, as indicated above. If only 1 percent of the $1.2 trillion in buying power is donated to churches, that would total about $12 billion annually.

A second way to estimate the total is by gleaning information from reports on African-American philanthropy. A report released in 2012 by the W. K. Kellogg Foundation and Rockefeller Philanthropy Advisors showed that nearly two-thirds of black households make charitable donations, worth a total of $11 billion a year. In fact, the study shows African-American donors give away higher percentages of their incomes than do white donors.[17] The majority of these donations were made to black churches, putting the total at a minimum of $6 billion annually.

A third method of determining the total annual income of black churches is to utilize previously determined proportions of charitable donations made by African Americans when compared with their total collective income. Target Market News conducts annual studies of black buying power, and its results have shown that African Americans spend about 3.5 percent of their total collective income on contributions.[18] By applying that percentage to the current total income of $1.2 trillion and then assuming about 60 percent of those funds go to black churches, the resultant amount would be about $25 billion.

Whichever method is used to calculate the total annual income of black churches, it is clear that the amount is substantial. When the black church is a conduit for transferring billions of dollars from African-American households to institutions and businesses from other ethnic communities, both the financial and political foundations of the black community are weakened. Increasing the amount of wealth retained could have life altering economic consequences for thousands of African Americans in urban areas across the United States through job creation, neighborhood revitalization, and infrastructure development.

The Growth in Church Income

The history of the African-American church is as old as the history of this nation. Established in 1777, the First African Baptist Church of Savannah, Georgia, is said to be the oldest black church in North America.[19] For the next nearly 200 years, black churches would remain relatively small, with localized congregations drawn from a radius of a few miles. These small congregations operated on limited budgets, and members paid "dues"—whatever they could afford out of their meager budgets. In rural areas, a pastor would often oversee two or three separate congregations as a single church could not afford to pay a preacher enough to earn a decent living. The pastor would minister on the first Sunday of the month at one church, the second Sunday at another, and so forth. Each congregation might have 50 to 100 members, many of them related by blood or marriage.

New York's Abyssinian Baptist Church, which became the nation's leading black house of worship under Pastor Adam Clayton Powell Jr., boasted 14,000 members in 1944 when Powell was first elected to Congress.[20] But in terms of church size, Abyssinian was the exception, not the rule, in the 1940s.

As educational and employment opportunities began to expand in the 1960s, membership at churches in traditional black communities began to grow and their budgets increased as a result. In large and medium-sized cities, church membership rolls of 500 to 1,000 or more became commonplace.

By the early 1970s, several social and economic trends began taking shape that dramatically affected the financial position of the black church. First, there was monumental growth in the size of the black middle class, which emerged in the early twentieth century and increased dramatically after the Civil Rights Act of 1964. This growth continued into the 1970s, 1980s, and 1990s, in part because of the enforcement of anti-discrimination laws in employment, but also due to increased educational opportunities.[21]

In 1960 only 20 percent of the black population completed high school and only 3 percent graduated from college. By 1980 over 50 percent of African Americans had graduated from high school, and 8 percent had graduated from college. In 2006, 86 percent of blacks between ages 25 and 29 had graduated from high school, and 19 percent had completed a bachelor's degree.[22] As a result of this economic shift, black parishioners increased the amount of their church tithes and offerings.

Second, the migration of the black middle class out of the inner cities to suburbs and outlying cities led to the expansion in the number of black churches. From 1960 to 2000, 9 million African Americans migrated from the inner cities to the suburbs. From 1990 to 2000, the percentage of African Americans living in suburbs increased to a total of 39 percent, rising 5 percent in that decade.[23]

The 2010 Census revealed that the migration from some of America's largest cities was substantial. Chicago's population fell by 200,418 from 2000 to 2010, and blacks accounted for almost 89 percent of that drop. Meanwhile, Plainfield, a Chicago suburb, grew by 204 percent overall, with its black population soaring by more than 2000 percent, the fastest rate in the region.[24]

The city of Atlanta showed a similar migration pattern during that decade as well as the city's black population fell by 29,746. During that period, the black population of the broader Atlanta metropolitan area, which includes suburban enclaves like Lithonia, Stone Mountain, and College Park, rose by 40 percent, an addition of 490,982.[25]

The San Francisco/Oakland, California, metropolitan area also experienced out-migration, losing 33,003 black residents between 2000 and 2010, a decline of 8 percent.[26] Several majority-black suburbs presently exist in the U.S., including Randallstown, Md.; College Park, Ga.; Hempstead, N.Y.; Forest Park, Ohio; and Missouri City, Texas.[27]

With the expansion of the black population to the suburbs, a demand was created for churches to be established in proximity to black middle class residents. Rather than drive long distances to attend church, some parishioners preferred not to commute to church every Sunday morning. Although membership rolls decreased at many inner-city churches, this migration led to an increase in the overall number of black churches. Dr. Amos C. Brown, pastor of Third Baptist Church in San Francisco, described the city's populous as "the rich, the immigrant poor, and that's it—no black middle class" in a *USA Today* interview. Brown sees the effects in his own church and in other black congregations.[28]

In addition, as white and multi-ethnic congregations have become more welcoming to black members, inner-city churches have been negatively impacted. As the black middle class has migrated to the suburbs, a growing number of worshippers have chosen to join churches with multi-ethnic congregations, some of which are shepherded by black pastors.

Dr. Michael W. Armstrong, senior pastor of the Colesville United Methodist Church (www.cumc.org) in Silver Spring, Maryland, is an example. Armstrong holds degrees from both Hampton University and Howard University, and his 400-member congregation is only 65 percent African American and African, with the remainder being mostly Caucasian.

The church, which was founded in the 1700s, is one of the oldest churches in the area. For centuries, Colesville had an all-white congregation in what was largely a rural area. But as the Washington, D.C., metropolitan area expanded and more black residents moved to Silver Spring, the church's membership gradually diversified.

Emphasis on Tithing

Prior to the 1960s and the expansion of the black middle class, few black churches emphasized tithing—giving 10 percent of one's income to the church—to support church operations. Most black families were barely able to make ends meet, and church contributions were based on whatever families could afford to give.

As church memberships began to grow in the 1970s, pastors began to place emphasis on tithing and encouraged their congregants to use that as a guideline for giving. Some within the prosperity ministry tied the giving of tithes and offerings to a future financial benefit for the donor. Church incomes ballooned as a result, making this a third factor in the increase in church contributions.

Emergence of Megachurches

A fourth factor in the increase in church incomes over the past four decades is the emergence of megachurches—ministries with congregations exceeding 10,000 members. Megachurches generate millions of dollars in annual income and have millions of dollars in assets. They also construct houses of worship that seat 3,000 or more people as well as other ancillary buildings, and they own dozens of acres of real estate. Some have multiple locations, either within the same city or in cities across the United States.

One of the earliest black megachurches, Crenshaw Christian Center in Los Angeles, was established in the 1970s by Rev. Frederick K. C. Price. Other nationally-known megachurches that have been established for at least two decades include the Potter's House led by Bishop T. D. Jakes (Dallas, Tex.), World Changers Church International pastored by Creflo Dollar Jr. (College Park, Ga.), New Light Christian Center Church led by Bishop I. V. Hilliard

(Houston, Tex.), and West Angeles Church of God in Christ pastored by Bishop Charles E. Blake (Los Angeles). However, nearly every large or medium-sized city with a significant black population includes at least one or two megachurches.

Utilization of Major Media Advertising

A final factor in the increase in church incomes is the utilization of radio and television advertising to market pastors' messages to the general public outside of their actual church walls. In the 1970s, black churches began to advertise on the radio by broadcasting their Sunday services to their local communities. These broadcasts helped attract new members and also solicited donations, both of which increased church income.

In the 1980s, some churches began to advertise on local television, and those with large church budgets broadcast nationally. The broadcasts usually included a sermon; advertising for books, audiotapes, or DVDs on a variety of scriptural topics; and the solicitation of donations. As a result, churches received income nationally (and sometimes internationally), which also expanded their donor base.

Some pastors even became radio station owners. Bishop Levi E. Willis Sr., president of Willis Broadcasting in the Tidewater area of Virginia, purchased his first station in 1974 and eventually owned more than a dozen stations nationwide, including the states of Alabama, Arkansas, Florida, Georgia, Illinois, Indiana, Louisiana, North Carolina, and Virginia. Willis was also the majority stockholder of Atlantic National Bank and in a funeral home and had ownership interests in motels and in *The Journal and Guide*, the black newspaper that served the Tidewater area for several decades.[29]

At the height of Willis' success in the 1980s, he owned 23 radio stations. In the 1990s, Willis experienced mounting problems with tax liens filed by the Internal Revenue Service, lawsuits, and financial mismanagement, which led to his company's demise. He passed away in 2009 at the age of 79 but was considered by many to be among the most influential black individuals in the area.[30]

Bishop Roy L. H. Winbush of Lafayette, Louisiana, and Bishop S. D. Johnson of Winston-Salem, North Carolina, each owned a radio station in their respective cities.[31] Bishop Samuel L. Green Jr. of Hampton, Va., owned a locally based religious TV station, WJCB-TV.[32] All four ministers—Willis, Winbush, Johnson, and Green—were leaders in the Church of God in Christ (COGIC) denomination.

CHAPTER 4

WEALTH TRANSFER BEGINS ON MONDAY MORNING

After Sunday offering receipts are counted and totaled, the wealth transfer begins on Monday morning when churches place their deposits in financial institutions, few of which are owned by African Americans. This is not surprising since, according to Federal Reserve data, there are only 22 banks with majority African-American ownership in the entire country, the lowest number in the last 150 years.[33] The sad reality is that even if black churches wanted to do business with a black-owned financial institution, they would not likely have access to one within their geographic area. But this was not always the case.

During their peak between the end of the Reconstruction era and the start of the Great Depression, more than 130 black-owned banks opened for business, providing capital to black entrepreneurs and prospective homeowners at a time when it was expensive or impossible to obtain elsewhere.[34] Black-owned banks suffered alongside their peers during each of America's economic downturns, including the Panic of 1873 and the Great Depression. One of the oldest banks is the Mechanics and Farmers Bank, which opened in 1908 in Durham, N.C., and is the eighth largest black-owned bank, with nearly $3 million in assets.[35] [36]

Following the Great Depression, only nine black-owned banks had survived. Just five new banks organized between 1934 and 1951, according to one estimate, and others shut down.[37] However, black banks continued to be mainstays in many black communities. Although the economic strategies of the civil rights movement are de-emphasized, leaders during this era understood the importance of banking where the impact of those dollars would benefit black communities.

During Dr. Martin Luther King Jr.'s final public speech, in Memphis, Tenn., the day before his assassination, he encouraged black residents to move their money to the city's black-owned bank. "I call upon you to take your money out of the banks downtown and deposit your money in Tri-State Bank," he said during his April 3, 1968, address. "We want a 'bank-in' movement in Memphis," said King, adding that the Southern Christian Leadership Conference had an account in the local black-owned savings and loan association. "We're telling you to follow what we're doing," said King, leading by example.[38]

Through efforts of the federal government in the 1970s via the Minority Bank Deposit Program and measures by the

Comptroller of the Currency, black banking experienced a resurgence.[39] But the renaissance became a victim of racial integration as black banks experienced the same loss in their customer base as did other black-owned institutions.

In 1986 there were 44 black-owned banks; in 2007 there were only 41. Consolidated Bank & Trust of Richmond, Va., was one of the banks that merged with another during this period and ceased its African-American majority ownership. The bank was originally founded as St. Luke Penny Savings Bank in 1903 by Maggie Walker (not to be confused with Madam C. J. Walker, the first black woman millionaire), the nation's first female of any race to become a bank CEO and the first African-American woman to run a bank. Prior to being acquired by Premier Financial Bancorp, Consolidated was also at one time known as the oldest continually African-American-operated bank in the country.[40]

After the economic collapse of 2008, the number of banks was down to only 23, which is less than one-half of 1 percent of all U.S. banks.[41] As of July 2016 there were only 22. Moreover, these banks are located in only 16 states.

One of the banks, Illinois Service Federal Savings and Loan Association (ISF), sought capital to revive its struggling operations and was acquired by a Ghanaian firm in May 2016. Groupe Nduom of Ghana invested $9 million in ISF, and the acquisition was expected to provide support to

Ghanaian businesses in the Chicago area.[42] During the same month the state of Wisconsin lost one of its two African-American-owned banks, North Milwaukee State Bank.[43]

Once the only option in their communities, America's black banks are now competing side by side with behemoths like Chase, Citibank, Wells Fargo, and Bank of America as well as with regional and local banks. Black churches are no different than other entities that are looking for the best banking opportunity available, but church leaders often consider utilizing black-owned banks whenever possible. Because of the dearth of black-owned financial institutions, in most cases, opening and maintaining an account is not possible nor practical due to geographic considerations.

There are no identifiable research studies that have measured the percentage of black churches that hold accounts at black banks. Furthermore, none of the pastors interviewed for this book lead churches whose primary accounts are held at a black-owned bank. However, Rev. Kevin Wayne Johnson, senior pastor of Accokeek First Church of God in Accokeek, Md., has a personal account at Baltimore's black-owned Harbor Bank. Johnson has been pleased with the bank's customer service, convenient location, and online banking services.

The Progressive National Baptist Convention is a Washington, D.C.-based organization that boasts 1.5 million members nationwide and represents about 5,000 black churches primarily in the United States. The Convention does not bank exclusively with African-American financial institutions, but it has accounts in two black-owned banks: Citizens Bank & Trust in Nashville, Tenn., and Industrial Bank in Washington, D.C.

According to the organization's general secretary Dr. Timothy Boddie, the Convention has been pleased with the services provided at both banks, but especially Citizens Bank. "They provided a level of special support as well as a line of credit that was difficult to get in relationships with other banks," Boddie said.

But churches can sometimes have mixed results in attempts to do business with black-owned banks. One African-American pastor in Houston who preferred not to be identified had hoped to do business with a black-owned bank in January 2013 when his 100-plus-member congregation purchased land to build its new sanctuary. The pastor's intention was to make a black-owned bank his church's primary financial institution.

However, at the time discussions with bank officials were underway, media reports surfaced that the bank was being investigated by federal bank officials for errors in its reporting practices. After hearing these reports, the pastor and church leaders decided to bank elsewhere. When a potential client is not 100 percent certain of doing business with a company and then hears negative reports, it can have a chilling effect on patronage for years to come. That is why it is vitally important that black-owned banks retain a high level of integrity, professionalism, and customer service.

Why Is "Banking Black" Important?

Access to capital is one of the primary reasons why supporting black banks is essential for both black churches and consumers. Statistics show that a qualified black borrower has a higher probability of getting his or her loan approved at a black bank, which means doing business with these institutions is a no-brainer.[44]

Teri Williams, president of the nation's largest black-owned financial institution, OneUnited Bank, explained why what she calls "banking black" is important in an address to members of Boston's Jubilee Christian Church on September 10, 2016. "In a period of a few weeks," she said, "our community moved $10 million to OneUnited Bank. This is part protest and part progress."

The protest part of the movement of these funds was prompted by the fatal shooting of two black men by police officers in Minnesota and Louisiana during the summer of 2016. Several celebrities—including hip hop artist Killer Mike; pop artists Usher, Alicia Keyes and Solange Knowles; and actor Jesse Williams—led by example and publicly encouraged others to do the same. As a result, the hashtags #bankblack and #blackdollarsmatter emerged, and thousands of black consumers followed suit.[45]

The progress part of the movement occurs because as black banks build their assets, they are able to provide loans to businesses and consumers in the neighborhoods that they serve. "The goal of the Bank Black movement is not just to get people to move their money but also to move their minds," said Teri Williams, who compared the assets at OneUnited Bank, which total $650 million, to the assets of the nation's largest Asian-American and Hispanic-American banks. "The largest Asian-American bank [East West Bancorp, based in Pasadena, California][46] has $33 billion in assets and the largest Hispanic American bank [International Bank of Commerce, based in Laredo, Texas] has $20 billion, so we have a long way to go to reach some sort of parity," she said.

Following is a complete list of U.S. African-American-owned banks as of September 2016:

Bank	Location
Alamerica Bank	Birmingham, Alabama
Commonwealth National Bank	Mobile, Alabama
Broadway Federal Bank	Los Angeles, California
Industrial Bank	Washington, D.C.
Carver State Bank	Savannah, Georgia

Citizens Trust Bank	Atlanta, Georgia
Illinois Service Federal Savings	Chicago, Illinois
Seaway Bank & Trust	Chicago, Illinois
Liberty Bank & Trust	New Orleans, Louisiana
Harbor Bank of Maryland	Baltimore, Maryland
OneUnited Bank	Boston, Massachusetts
First Independence Bank	Detroit, Michigan
City National Bank of New Jersey	Newark, New Jersey
Carver Federal Savings	New York, New York
Mechanics & Farmers Bank	Durham, North Carolina
United Bank of Philadelphia	Philadelphia, Pennsylvania
South Carolina Community Bank	Columbia, South Carolina
Citizens Savings Bank & Trust	Nashville, Tennessee
Tri-State Bank of Memphis	Memphis, Tennessee
Unity National Bank of Houston	Houston, Texas
First State Bank	Danville, Virginia
Columbia Savings & Loan	Milwaukee, Wisconsin

There are also more than 300 black-owned credit unions nationwide that provide financial services to their members. Credit unions operate differently than banks and, for this reason, are generally not utilized as a depository for church funds.

Credit unions differ from banks in a variety of ways. First, credit union members are owners, have voting rights, and can run for election to the board. Banks' depositors are customers and have no ownership interest in the institution. Banks are owned and controlled by stockholders and customers have no voting rights.[47]

Second, credit unions are local and are organized to serve the interests of their memberships. Banks, conversely, are open to the general public. Third, credit unions are not-for-profit financial cooperatives, whereas banks are for-profit corporations with declared earnings paid to stockholders only.

Fourth, credit unions focus on consumer loans and member savings; banks focus on commercial loans and accounts and services that generate significant income. Finally, credit union deposits are federally insured by the National Credit Union Administration (NCUA), while bank deposit accounts are insured by the Federal Deposit Insurance Corporation (FDIC). Deposits for both credit unions and banks are insured up to $250,000.[48]

More than 100 black churches nationwide have established credit unions as arms of their ministries, and some have been in operation for more than 60 years. Although all credit unions do not offer the same menu of services, most provide an array of services, including checking and savings accounts, auto loans, credit cards, mortgages, home equity loans, and financial literacy classes.

Some provide scholarships to children of credit union members.

A comprehensive list of more than 120 black churches with established federal credit unions is shown below. About 67 percent of these credit unions have assets less than $500,000, and only about 17 percent have assets exceeding $1 million. Still, these credit unions represent long-term success in pooling financial resources within local communities to provide access to loans and other services that may be lacking.[49]

Church Name	Year C.U. Established	Location
New Pilgrim Baptist Church	1965	Birmingham, AL
Saint John AME Church	1958	Birmingham, AL
Sixth Avenue Baptist Church	1963	Birmingham, AL
People's Independent Church of Christ	1956	Los Angeles, CA
Zion Hill Baptist Church	1969	Los Angeles, CA
Calvary Baptist Church of Pacoima	1973	San Fernando, CA
Bethel AME Church	1969	San Francisco, CA
Jones Methodist Church	1953	San Francisco, CA
Faith Tabernacle Baptist Church	1956	Stamford, CT
First Baptist Church (Stratford)	1974	Stratford, CT
Immanuel Baptist Church	1981	New Haven, CT
East End Baptist Tabernacle	1982	Bridgeport, CT
John Wesley AME Zion Church	1976	Washington, DC
Mount Airy Baptist Church	1985	Washington, DC
Mount Gilead Baptist Church	1950	Washington, DC
Mount Jezreel Baptist Church	1986	Washington, DC
Paramount Baptist Church	1983	Washington, DC

St. Gabriel Catholic Church	1967	Washington, DC
Saint James AME Church	1957	Miami, FL
Florida Conference AME		
Church	1976	Tallahassee, FL
Tabernacle Baptist Church	1961	Augusta, GA
Big Bethel AME Church	1995	Atlanta, GA
First African Baptist Church	1954	Savannah, GA
Bethel AME Church	1974	Chicago, IL
Fellowship Baptist Church	1977	Chicago, IL
Greater Institutional AME		
Church	1958	Chicago, IL
Israel Methodist Community		
Church	1963	Chicago, IL
Park Manor Christian Church	1955	Chicago, IL
Pilgrim Baptist Church	1953	Chicago, IL
Resurrection Lutheran Church	1962	Chicago, IL
Saint Elizabeth Parish	1944	Chicago, IL
Saint Helena Parish	1984	Chicago, IL
Saint Mark United Methodist		
Church	1954	Chicago, IL
Saint Martin De Porres Parish	1960	Chicago, IL
Shiloh Baptist Church		
(Englewood)	1963	Chicago, IL
Trinity United Church of Christ	1978	Chicago, IL
Antioch Missionary Baptist		
Church	1970	Decatur, IL
Canaan Baptist Church	2001	Urbana, IL
Gideon Missionary Baptist		
Church	1998	Waukegan, IL
Shiloh Baptist Church	1963	Waukegan, IL
Mount Zion Missionary Baptist		
Church	1987	Zion, IL
Union Baptist Church	2006	Fort Wayne, IN
Saint Monica & Luke Church	1953	Gary, IN

Mount Zion Baptist Church	1963	Indianapolis, IN
Bethel AME Church	1982	Baton Rouge, LA
Church of God in Christ (COGIC)	1981	Lafayette, LA
Immaculate Heart of Mary Catholic Church	1942	Lafayette, LA
Avenue Baptist Church	1957	Shreveport, LA
Mount Lebanon Baptist Church	1970	Baltimore, MD
Reid Temple AME Church	2006	Glenn Dale, MD
Messiah Baptist - Jubilee Church	1983	Brockton, MA
Bethel AME Church	1936	Detroit, MI
Bethel Baptist Church East	1974	Detroit, MI
Greater Christ Baptist Church	1957	Detroit, MI
Greater New Mount Moriah Baptist Church	1968	Detroit, MI
New Rising Star Missionary Baptist Church	1983	Detroit, MI
West Side Baptist Church	1974	Saint Louis, MO
First Baptist Church	1944	Cranford, NJ
Messiah Baptist Church	1973	East Orange, NJ
Salem Baptist Church	1962	Jersey City, NJ
Israel Memorial AME Church	1956	Newark, NJ
Heard AME Church	1980	Roselle, NJ
Beulah Church of the Nazarene	2007	Brooklyn, NY
Cornerstone Baptist Church	1957	Brooklyn, NY
Bethel AME Church	1950	Buffalo, NY
Saint John Baptist Church	1973	Buffalo, NY
First Baptist Church	1975	East Elmhurst, NY
Varick Memorial AME Church	1997	Hempstead, NY
Greater Centennial AME Zion Church	1969	Mount Vernon, NY
Macedonia Baptist Church	1960	Mount Vernon, NY
Abyssinian Baptist Church	1940	New York, NY

All Souls Episcopal Church	1953	New York, NY
Church of the Master	1944	New York, NY
Grace Congregational Church		
of Harlem	1952	New York, NY
Saint Philip's Church	1951	New York, NY
Southern Baptist Church of		
New York	1978	New York, NY
Union Congregational Church	1948	New York, NY
Saint John AME Church	1968	Niagara Falls, NY
Union Baptist Church –		
Greenburgh	1965	White Plains, NY
Mount Vernon Baptist Church	1948	Durham, NC
Mount Zion of Woodlawn		
Baptist Church	1968	Cincinnati, OH
Cleveland Church of Christ	1975	Cleveland, OH
Cory Methodist Church	1958	Cleveland, OH
Greater Abyssinia Baptist		
Church	1959	Cleveland, OH
Lane Metropolitan CME		
Church	2016	Cleveland, OH
Saint Paul AME Zion Church	Unknown	Cleveland, OH
Bethany Baptist Christian		
Church	1983	Chester, PA
Morning Star Baptist Church	1972	Clairton, PA
First Baptist Church of Darby	1980	Darby, PA
Allen AME Church	1984	Philadelphia, PA
Bright Hope Baptist Church	1958	Philadelphia, PA
Canaan Baptist Church	1976	Philadelphia, PA
Holsey Temple CME Church	1966	Philadelphia, PA
Holy Trinity Baptist Church	1966	Philadelphia, PA
Mount Airy Baptist Church	1986	Philadelphia, PA
Mount Carmel Baptist Church	1964	Philadelphia, PA
Pinn Memorial Baptist Church	1965	Philadelphia, PA
Saint Paul's Baptist Church	1968	Philadelphia, PA

Sharon Baptist Church	2003	Philadelphia, PA
Wayland Temple Baptist Church	1975	Philadelphia, PA
Wesley AME Zion Church	1961	Philadelphia, PA
White Rock Baptist Church	1978	Philadelphia, PA
First African Baptist Church	1978	Sharon Hill, PA
Trinity Baptist Church	1969	Florence, SC
Mount Olive Baptist Church	1997	Arlington, TX
Friendship-West Baptist Church	1959	Dallas, TX
Good Street Baptist Church	1957	Dallas, TX
Oak Cliff Bible Fellowship	2008	Dallas, TX
Brentwood Baptist Church	1993	Houston, TX
New Light Christian Center Church	2004	Houston, TX
Our Mother of Mercy Catholic Church	1965	Houston, TX
Mount Pleasant Baptist Church	2000	Alexandria, VA
Queen Street Baptist Church	1969	Hampton, VA
New Bethel Baptist Church	1978	Portsmouth, VA
Fifth Street Baptist Church	1970	Richmond, VA
Trinity Baptist Church	1998	Richmond, VA
High Street Baptist Church	1957	Roanoke, VA
Metropolitan Church	1949	Suffolk, VA
First Baptist Church of Vienna	1995	Vienna, VA
Northwest Baptist Church	1958	Seattle, WA
Greater Galilee Baptist Church	1965	Milwaukee, WI
Holy Redeemer Church of God in Christ	1993	Milwaukee, WI

What Banks Do With Deposits

To understand the reverberating effects of African-American churches moving their funds to other communities every week, one must understand what happens when money is deposited into a bank. First, deposits are counted as both assets and liabilities for the financial institution. As an asset, deposits increase a bank's market value and can be used as collateral for a bank's expansion or capital acquisitions.[50] As a liability, the bank owes the depositor the money upon request, but rarely do churches withdraw all of the funds in their bank account unless the account is being closed.

This means that the bank has access to the deposits, after setting aside a certain percentage as reserves, to lend money to customers and earn interest on the loans. The Federal Reserve sets what is called the reserve ratio, which is the percentage of any deposit that is required to be retained by the bank. Higher reserve ratios make banks safer, but they also make banks less profitable since it means they have less money to make loans.[51]

Redlining Still Exists

Lending money carries a certain amount of risk, but banks mitigate the risk by researching the credit worthiness of potential borrowers. Ironically, money deposited by African-American churches could then subsequently be used to deny loans to African-American consumers or to charge them higher interest rates. Historically, banks have been less willing to make loans to black consumers, and, unfortunately, discrimination in lending practices—also known as "redlining"—still exists.

Federal regulators and the U.S. Justice Department found that, during the housing bubble, minority borrowers were pushed into costlier subprime loans or charged higher fees than comparable white borrowers. When the housing market collapsed and the financial crisis exploded, the result was that the average income in nonwhite or Hispanic families fell by 11 percent during the three-year period afterward.[52] In addition, black people held 5.2 percent of the nation's home loans in 2014, compared with 8.7 percent in 2006.[53] Although the practice was outlawed decades ago, redlining has re-emerged as a serious concern among regulators as banks have dramatically retreated from providing home loans to African Americans in the wake of the financial crisis.[54]

As is the case with much of racial discrimination in the 2000s, redlining has evolved and is no longer obvious but is instead subtle. Rather than overtly deny loans to black people, some banks quietly have bias built in to their operations by placing branches and mortgage services outside minority communities.[55] Meanwhile, payday and auto title loan companies, which charge notoriously high interest rates, proliferate in those neighborhoods.

To highlight the menace that banking discrimination still harbors, BancorpSouth, Inc. settled a lawsuit for $10.6 million in June 2016 under which the bank was being sued for encouraging discriminatory mortgage lending practices.

The U.S. Department of Justice concluded that the bank, which has operations in Mississippi, Arkansas, and Tennessee, used racial criteria to direct potential borrowers toward certain neighborhoods and determined their eligibility for loans.[56]

In addition, BancorpSouth evaded areas with large African-American populations by refraining from opening branches or allocating those areas to loan officers. The settlement includes $2.78 million paid to black consumers who were illegally denied or overcharged for their loans. Citigroup Inc., JPMorgan Chase & Co., Bank of America Corp., and Deutsche Bank AG have all been sued in recent years for discrimination in lending practices.

Wells Fargo was named in a class-action lawsuit filed by the NAACP due to the bank's discriminatory practices. According to a Wells Fargo loan officer, Beth Jacobson, the bank had an "emerging-markets unit that specifically targeted black churches, because it figured church leaders had a lot of influence and could convince congregants to take out subprime loans," she told the *New York Times*.[57]

When wealth leaves the hands of African-American consumers, is placed in church collection plates, and is immediately deposited into banks without black ownership, many of those funds can actually be used to discriminate against the very people who are building the assets of the white-owned financial institution. The economics of the nature of wealth transfer through black churches to banks that may be unfriendly or even hostile is a peculiar paradox that goes largely unnoticed.

CHAPTER 5

MORTGAGES, INTEREST PAYMENTS, LEASES, UTILITIES, AND OTHER COMMON CHURCH EXPENDITURES

Once church bank deposits are made, where do churches spend their money? This is a question many parishioners have likely never contemplated in a collective sense, although they may have done so for their individual churches. But the spending categories play an important role in the wealth transfer process, and identifying these categories can greatly assist in the movement of funds to black institutions and enterprises.

The next phase of wealth transfer commences as the funds are disbursed to separate entities and vendors. According to Dr. Claud Anderson, in his book, *PowerNomics*, nearly 99 percent of money spent by black churches passes into the white community through mortgage payments, insurance premiums, television and radio advertising costs, printing expenses, maintenance, utilities, and so forth.[58]

For church expenditures, an annual budget may be voted on by a majority within the church body, but the decision about which vendors are actually used is likely made using a variety of methods. The decision regarding which financial institutions or vendors are used may be made unilaterally by the pastor, jointly by the pastor and a finance committee, or by the pastor and the deacon board or trustee board. At most black churches, the pastor has some latitude regarding using a particular vendor within a certain dollar range.

There are four major categories of financial obligations that nearly all churches expend and which comprise a substantial portion of a church budget: mortgages, interest on debt, building leases, and utilities. Depending on the size of the membership, the church may or may not have paid staff members, and for smaller churches with less than 100 members, the pastor may not be considered a full-time employee in terms of paid hours.

A church body requires a meeting place. That is usually, but not always, a church building. The church sanctuary may be one built by members of the church and which requires a mortgage financed by a bank or mortgage company that is rarely black-owned. The mortgage is paid over a period of decades, and interest is paid on the debt. As is the case with mortgages generally, the amount of interest paid over time may far exceed the principal.

Many churches are constantly in a building mode, adding extensions to their main sanctuaries or building ancillary structures, such as community centers or family life centers. This construction is rarely paid for in cash, and a mortgage is required to finance building completion. Depending on the buildings' square footage, mortgage and interest expenses can total thousands—or even millions—of dollars annually. Unlike residential mortgages, many church mortgages are structured with monthly payments during the early years of the loan and a balloon payment to pay off the remaining loan amount or refinance the amount for a new term.[59]

For new churches that are in their infancy, members may meet in one of the organizers' designated homes until enough funds are available to lease property or a meeting space. A meeting location will often be in a strip center or a school. Some new churches will utilize the church sanctuaries of other established churches during hours when the buildings are not in use.

Rev. Henry Prosper, pastor of Westfield Community Baptist Church (www.westfieldcbc.com) in Houston, Texas, established the church in 2008 and has leased office space for several years. Westfield currently has a 300-seat sanctuary under construction that is expected to be completed in 2017. Prosper said it is challenging for small churches to grow to a substantial size in terms of membership without being in a traditional church building. "In the minds of a lot of people, a church is not real unless it is in a church facility," he said.

Some older, well-established churches, like the Accokeek First Church of God in Accokeek, Maryland, own their property outright. Accokeek was built in 1956 and is situated on a three-acre plot. The church building, land, and two single-family homes—one of which is the church parsonage—are all clear from mortgages, says its senior pastor, Rev. Kevin Wayne Johnson, who was installed in 2014.

The Progressive National Baptist Convention is in a unique position of owning its 50th Street headquarters in Northeast Washington, D.C., outright. Its offices are housed in a building first purchased by noted educator and orator Nannie Helen Burroughs in the early 1900s, according to the organization's general secretary, Dr. Timothy Boddie.

Born in 1879, Burroughs was an educator, orator, religious leader, and businesswoman who moved to Washington, D.C., as a young woman to take advantage of the city's superior educational opportunities. While living in the nation's capital, she decided to open a school for African-American girls to prepare them for a productive life. The school, opened in 1909, was called the National Training School for Women and Girls, but was renamed the Nannie Helen Burroughs School in 1964.[60]

In addition to the mortgages, interest payments, and leases that comprise a church's largest financial obligations, churches make monthly utility payments for electricity, gas and water to their local utility companies. Depending on the size of the church and the amount of square footage of church buildings, utility payments can range from a few hundred to several thousand dollars per month. For the most part, utilities are regulated monopolies, many are publicly traded, and I was unable to identify a single one in the U.S. that is majority black-owned.

Other Common Church Expenditures

When black churches have paid staff members— including the pastor, administrative staff, maintenance workers, etc.—wealth transfer is at least realized through one cycle. This means that the funds collected from black parishioners that go toward the salaries of black staff members transfer at least one time before leaving the hands of black consumers entirely.

However, many churches that have small congregations of 100 members or less have no paid staff members at all. Even the pastor may not be a paid employee or may be only considered part-time with little to no benefits. Smaller congregations depend heavily upon the volunteer efforts of their members. Yet there are some categories of ongoing or one-time expenditures that churches often require, and the amounts tend to be substantial. Churches have few to zero options in terms of utilizing African-American-owned businesses for these expenditures, which include:

- **Insurance.** Property and vehicle insurance is usually underwritten by large multinational companies, like State Farm and Nationwide, although churches may utilize a black insurance agent to handle the transactions. Breath of Life Christian Center in Memphis, Tenn., for example, utilizes black agents for all of its insurance needs.

- **Construction/Contractors.** Local contractors are hired to provide services such as painting, roofing and A/C and heating maintenance. The building of new facilities or the construction of extensions to existing structures is handled by construction companies. Utilizing an experienced black-owned construction company or contractor may not be an option.

- **Furnishings.** Church pews, cushioned chairs, offering tables, communion tables, pulpits, lecterns, and/or cabinetry, are usually one-time, high-ticket items most churches will need when they lease or purchase a sanctuary building.

- **Choir robes and church uniforms.** Choir robes and uniforms for various church ministries and auxiliaries are standard fare at most black churches.

- **Sound systems and musical equipment.** Pianos, keyboards, organs, drums, guitars, amplifiers, and wireless and standing microphones are used to varying degrees, depending upon the size of the church.

- **Vehicle purchases and leases.** Church vans, buses, and cars are purchased or leased for church transportation purposes.

- **Communion cup wafer and juice sets.** Most churches observe the sacrament of Holy Communion at least once a month. Some churches serve the bread and wine separately, but many churches have adopted use of the sets.

- **Sunday school and Bible study materials.** Nearly all churches customarily hold Sunday school, Bible study, Vacation Bible School, and other regularly scheduled discipleship activities. Urban Ministries (www.urbanministries.com) is one of the few black-owned companies that provides church curriculum and educational materials.

- **Hymnals and Bibles.** Hymnals are not used by churches as much as they were in prior generations but are still in use at some churches. The King James Version of the Bible with a plain leather cover was the standard in years past, but versions with more modern language and imagery (e.g., New King James Version, Living Bible, Amplified Bible, and New International Version) are now commonly used. Urban Spirit (www.urbanspirit.biz) publishes special editions of the Bible specifically for children, women and men designed for people of color and is the only African-American owned publisher of Bibles in the U.S. According to the latest survey by Zondervan, African Americans owned 4.5 Bibles per household, compared to the national average of 3.9. About 65 percent of African Americans reported they read Bibles frequently, compared with the national average of 40 percent.[61] In addition, 29 percent of African Americans are considered Bible engaged, the most of any race.[62]

- **Advertising and Media.** Some churches spend thousands of dollars per year on television and radio advertising or broadcasting their church services or pastor's sermons on Christian broadcasting networks and cable television. For megachurches, million-dollar advertising budgets are not uncommon. One need only tune in during late night broadcasting on Black Entertainment Television (BET) to see back-to-back programs of ministers preaching a brief sermon, followed by the promotion of videos, books, and religious artifacts and requesting donations. Ironically, BET is no longer black-owned and was purchased by Viacom in 2000.[63] Radio One (www.radio-one.com) is a black-owned radio network that many churches utilize to promote their Sunday services and events.

Black churches appear to have greater opportunities to patronize black-owned companies for personalized services where these businesses are more commonplace and dollar commitment is smaller. These include the areas of printing, graphic design, photography, catering, website design, and landscaping. Some churches use independent entrepreneurs who do not have a formal, registered business but who provide services as a sideline, especially in the areas of catering and photography.

CHAPTER 6

IT'S EASIER SAID THAN DONE

At first glance, it would seem to be a simple proposition: If black churches simply made recirculating the dollars they receive from their parishioners a priority in terms of supporting black enterprises, the wealth transfer could easily be halted and reversed. While this is true theoretically, the reality is much more difficult and complex.

The Empowerment Experiment

Black churches encounter the same obstacles experienced by the Anderson family in Chicago, Illinois, when they embarked on a similar quest in 2009. Chronicled in the 2012 book by Maggie Anderson titled *Our Black Year: One Family's Quest to Buy Black in America's Racially Divided Economy*, this Chicago family publicly pledged to exclusively support black businesses and professionals for an entire year, an effort they called "The Ebony Experiment" when it was first launched. (They would later be forced to change the name, which will be explained later in this chapter.)[64] The Andersons' project received widespread national media coverage when they were featured on CNN,

MSNBC, *The Wall Street Journal*, and other major media outlets.

Chicago is one of America's largest cities, includes more than 1 million black residents, and has a rich history of black entrepreneurship. Yet, almost immediately, the Andersons discovered that the dearth of black-owned businesses that provided essential products and services was only a small part of the problem. In fact, the best word to describe their black year is "tortuous."

Maggie Anderson, the matriarch of this young couple's family, possesses an unparalleled commitment to wealth retention and group economics within black communities across the United States. The Chicago family went to great lengths to pursue this worthwhile goal, including purchasing gas cards from black-owned stations 40 to 50 miles away with the intention of redeeming them at gas stations closer to home. The couple had difficulty finding new clothes and shoes for their two small children because they could identify only one black-owned store that provided children's clothes: Jordan's Closets, a consignment shop. During the Andersons' year-long odyssey, they also discovered that purchasing essential household goods—like toiletries, cosmetics, and over-the-counter drugs—from a black-owned source was next to impossible.[65]

Although they anticipated broad community support when they initially launched the Experiment, even more challenging were the entrenched negative attitudes about black-owned companies held by most consumers, especially black ones. The Andersons also encountered political opposition, ambivalence from academics who were considered experts in urban planning and economic strategies, and even a threatened lawsuit from *Ebony* magazine because of their use of the word "ebony" in their project's title.

They initially had high hopes of support from *Ebony*, one of the nation's most important black-owned media entities. But two days after their project received front-page coverage in the *Chicago Tribune*, they received a heartbreaking email from *Ebony*'s legal department informing them that a lawsuit would be filed in federal court at the end of the day if they did not change the name of their project.[66]

There were also several unexpected and perplexing findings. First, the effort proved to be expensive. Because the Andersons wanted to make theirs a public effort, they incurred upfront expenses for their effort before it even got off the ground. They spent $5,000 developing a website, hiring academics to conduct an economic study, and building a directory of black-owned businesses. They were often required to drive dozens of miles out of their way to locate a black-owned business, only to discover upon arrival that the business had closed its doors, the product selection was extremely limited, the service or product was no longer available, or the facilities were unacceptable.

For example, one store they attempted to patronize, J's Fresh Meats, was not only "cramped, dirty, and a little foreboding, sort of like the way it feels to walk into an abandoned building" but it also stocked no meat at all—fresh or otherwise. Months later the Andersons made a trek to the store only to discover that, not surprisingly, its doors were closed permanently. They then drove 14 miles to another store, Woods Grocery on the South Side, which was only slightly more aesthetically appealing but with much higher prices. The Chicago couple also paid higher-than-usual prices for the same items they had purchased the previous year from local, non-black-owned companies.[67]

The second perplexing—even bizarre—phenomenon the Andersons experienced was that for some types of businesses, black consumers were *less* likely to patronize them if they found out the businesses were black-owned. Stated even more bluntly by Dr. Sammie Holloway, pastor of Breath of Life Christian Center in Memphis, Tenn., "Black people have been pointed in a direction where they automatically boycott black businesses." Holloway has spent more than a decade attempting to steer the 1,500 members of his church in the direction of group economics with limited results, which are detailed later in this chapter.

This knee-jerk rejection of black businesses by black consumers is a phenomenon I call *reverse group economics*, meaning that we spend our dollars elsewhere *first* before we consider spending our dollars with an enterprise within our own community. The practice of reverse group economics among African Americans had its beginnings five decades ago on the heels of the civil rights movement. The civil rights movement of the 1960s and the resultant equal rights legislation was certainly a much needed and hard fought victory. But the emphasis on racial integration that followed ushered in a period of extreme reverse group economics from which we have yet to recover.

Prior to the late 1960s, nearly every metropolitan and small-town area in the U.S. with a significant black population had a commercial area filled with black-owned shops, theaters, restaurants, hotels, and other business establishments. Some, like those in Durham, N.C., and Tulsa, Okla., in the 1920s were referred to as "Black Wall Street" because of the high level of commerce practiced in their black neighborhoods. The 1960s' emphasis on integration, with its underlying premise that all white-owned businesses were inherently superior to those owned by African Americans, shifted millions of dollars out of black communities and resulted in the closure of the majority of the existing businesses.

In fact, black consumers often only contact a black-owned business in one of three situations:

- When they are looking for a "hook-up" (a drastic reduction in customary prices);
- When they are looking for a donation; or
- When all other sources have been exhausted.

In many cases, it is considered a status symbol to patronize a multinational, billion-dollar corporation (not African-American owned) while repeatedly bypassing black entrepreneurs who can provide the same product or service. In Anderson's view, black consumers have an inclination to prove our worth by shopping at "white" stores, which is both a heavily promoted sign of our advancement as well as a reaction to the perceived lower-quality black businesses.[68]

Chicago's Black-Owned Grocery Store

In *Our Black Year*, Maggie Anderson details, with anguish, her crusade to get a black-owned grocery store on Chicago's predominantly black South Side. Unlike her experience with J's Fresh Meats, Maggie identified a top-of-the-line, black-owned grocery store, Farmers Best Market, which opened in 2009. Sadly, its proprietor, Karriem Beyah, met resistance from black residents, who failed to patronize the store despite its first-class ambiance and food selection.

"It was clean," writes Maggie. "It was bright. The produce was fresh. The selection of foods was wide. The employees were professional." Beyah kept his doors open as long as he could, but without customers, he simply could not survive.[69]

Unfortunately, advice Maggie unwittingly provided Beyah may have escalated the store's demise. With a law degree and MBA from the University of Chicago, Maggie's experience is in a corporate environment, and her worldview was the opposite of the approach Beyah would have needed to have any hopes of building a grocery business in a low-income black neighborhood.

First, she encouraged him to promote the store as a black-owned entity, and this was highlighted in his radio and print advertisements. This was an instance where the goals of the Empowerment Experiment were in direct conflict with the best interest of Farmers Best Market. Because of the negative image many black-owned businesses currently have, doing so actually meant consumers would avoid the store rather than patronize it. Both Maggie and Karriem realized this after it was too late. "If you're under the radar," he said, "then maybe you won't get that belief from customers that the other guy's ice is colder than yours."

Second, Maggie engineered a sponsorship by Farmers Best Market of the Real Men Cook Chicago picnic, a move that is the opposite of what a fledging start-up business should do. Sponsorship resources come from profits that are realized. When a business is just getting off the ground, it can ill afford to spend thousands of dollars to sponsor events when it has virtually no customer base. To do so is counterintuitive. Yet when Jewel, the largest grocery chain in the Chicago metropolitan area, with 185 stores, backed out at the last minute, Anderson thought sponsoring the event would be helpful.

Jewel is a decades-old, profitable business, and when it pulled out at the last minute, that was a clear sign that the store's management didn't believe the derived benefits were commensurate with the funds expended. Consumers need to develop a habit and pattern of spending money with a company *first*. When a business starts the consumer relationship by giving products away rather than selling them, it is difficult to change the dynamics of the relationship later. While Karriem received branding and logo prominence during Real Men Cook, he spent the day giving away coupons and free food.

Also, grocery stores market primarily by advertising products that are known as "loss leaders," items retailers use as inducements to get customers into their stores. This item(s) is usually sold below cost, or at a loss, to get foot traffic in the store. Customers will then, presumably, purchase other items at regular or higher profit margins.

Utilizing his resources to create and distribute a colorful weekly flyer of sale items or loss leaders to consumers within a five-mile radius of the store would have been a much more effective marketing strategy.

The Fate of Covenant Bank

Shortly after launching the Experiment, the Andersons moved their finances to the city's black-owned Covenant Bank. Maggie did not indicate that she had any challenges during her interactions with the bank in her book, but the institution has since closed its doors.

Ironically, Covenant was run by megachurch pastor Bill Winston and was closed in February 2013 by bank regulators, wiping out the investments of more than 3,000 members of Rev. Winston's Living Word Christian Center. Winston had long sought a bank to help put to the test his stated belief that godly pursuits lead to financial success. He hoped ownership of the lender would help revitalize West Side neighborhoods, where the bank was based. But the loans it provided quickly soured as the recession hit, depleting capital levels.[70]

Winston's ministry website highlights the following scripture:

> This is the regulation for the release: every creditor shall forgive what he has loaned to his neighbor; he shall not require repayment from his neighbor and his brother, because the Lord's release has been proclaimed. [Deuteronomy 15:22-AMP][71]

This Old Testament scripture is the exact opposite approach that a bank should use when lending money to consumers and businesses. It may succeed as a religious philosophy, but as Winston found, it is a recipe for disaster in the banking industry. Covenant's saga demonstrates the limits of a pastoral calling when extended to financial pursuits that require specific professional expertise. There is no substitute for hiring experienced executives to manage a major business operation.

Mistakes Were Made

The Andersons would be the first to acknowledge that, in hindsight, they made a number of mistakes during their yearlong quest. Maggie addressed most of their errors in the Appendix of her book in the section titled "Maggie's Tips for Buying Black the EE Way." In my view, although their intentions were noble, they made three crucial missteps during the Empowerment Experiment.

First, as the Andersons concluded, trying to spend all of their money with black-owned companies was virtually impossible. Their goal was completely unrealistic and led to frustration and discouragement. "We were optimistic and naïve enough to believe we could find what we needed," writes Maggie. In order for a business relationship to be sustainable over the long haul, doing business with a targeted company should be a pleasant, hassle-free experience. A better strategy is to direct one's spending for specific needs to black-owned firms that can fulfill your needs and develop a long-term relationship with them.

Maggie described the selection of these enterprises as choices among "low hanging fruit" or, in other words, spending money with those companies where you can alter your spending habits to purchase what is most convenient. Her suggestions were to "subscribe to a Black newspaper or magazine, support Black designers at the department stores, buy Black-made products at mass retailers and grocery stores, open an account at a Black-owned bank, buy gift cards at Black-owned McDonald's or Burger King."[72]

Unlike during the decades that included Reconstruction, Jim Crow, and forced segregation, black-owned businesses are no longer located exclusively in majority-black neighborhoods. But even for those businesses located in edge cities and suburbs, they are still more likely to hire black employees and utilize some black suppliers, thereby retaining black dollars in circulation among the black population for a longer period than is presently the case.

Avoid Mainstream Media Attention

Second, promoting the project through the mainstream media brought with it more minuses than pluses and nearly ensured its demise. Quietly conducting group economics may seem to be counterintuitive, but it is the most effective way for it to succeed. To succeed, it has to occur under the radar, undetected by the opposition. In fact, seeking attention through mainstream media should be avoided as this type of exposure will ultimately doom a group economics project to failure for several reasons.

Media attention invites opposition and a backlash. Maggie became keenly aware of this whenever she was interviewed on national television or was the subject of a feature story in a daily newspaper. When an article about the project appeared in the *Chicago Sun-Times* on December 20, 2008, the negative comments in response to the article, calling the Andersons racists and worse, brought her to tears. "It was hurtful and fearful being called a racist, a Nazi and the N-word, as well as having death threats and hate mail sent to my house," she said in a presentation on group economics at Jubilee Baptist Church in September 2016.

The reaction to a front-page story about the project that appeared in the March 9 edition of the *Chicago Tribune* was similar. "More than twenty-one hundred comments were posted to the *Tribune*'s online version of the story, and an additional one hundred-plus emails were sent directly to the paper," writes Maggie. "The vast majority was critical, contending that we were engaging in racism." A man in Oregon even started a Facebook group opposing what was then called the Ebony Experiment.[73]

The project's website also received its share of angry emails from white people who had read about their objectives and considered their motives to be racist. One couple wrote, "Why not go all the way, Andersons, and move the hell back to Africa. Take your daughters with you." Others were much worse and included expletives with accompanying graphics.[74]

It is a near certainty that individuals from other ethnic groups will misunderstand the objectives and intentions underlying efforts to pursue group economics among African Americans. Economic activity that nearly every ethnic group (except African Americans) routinely engages in is viewed as blatant racism when exercised by black people. In fact, even a substantial portion of the black population will neither understand this concept nor support it. The Andersons were taken aback by the response from black callers during a three-hour appearance on the nationally-syndicated Doug Banks radio show in August 2009. (Doug Banks passed away in April 2016.)

The topic of the show was "Should Black People Do More to Support Black Businesses?" and, writes Maggie,

"We got our answer in a hurry: no bleeping way." She further described the lack of like-mindedness among those who called the show. "Only one caller supported self-help economics and pledged to do more to spend his money at local, Black businesses. The rest tore apart the ideals behind our mission, usually by recounting a story about a disappointing experience at a Black business and then swearing off ever patronizing one again."[75]

The Andersons appeared to be unprepared for the reality that not everybody would share their vision. Like the Andersons, others who pursue the objective of group economics will find that even among black people, most will be ambivalent, and some will even be hostile. But those who have similar goals and a level of consciousness will understand, encourage, and spread the word. Social media is a more effective communication vehicle to target those with similar aspirations, outside of the watchful eyes of those who feel threatened by a raised level of consciousness among African Americans regarding economic matters.

Another reason to avoid mainstream media is that it ignites the "crab syndrome," or the widely touted concept that when a black person appears to be successful, similar to crabs in a bucket, other black people will try to pull that person down. Unfortunately, the crab syndrome is not a myth but a reality. There are many black people who will see the

69

Andersons, or someone else with similar goals, on national television and oppose their efforts simply because they are getting national exposure. They could care less about the viability of the idea or the jobs that could be created. They allow envy to consume them and seek to undermine rather than uplift. Some people simply do not want to see another black person do well, especially if they are not.

A different manifestation of the crab syndrome is that opportunists, copycats, and those with personal agendas will come out of the woodwork, especially if they believe they can receive their fifteen minutes of fame by attempting to duplicate the efforts of another person. These opportunists have no genuine interest in promoting group economics; they are simply attention seekers pursuing their time in the spotlight.

Still another manifestation of the crab syndrome is the lack of support from influence makers—prominent individuals who one would think would be fully supportive of group economics but, for whatever reason, choose to sit on the sidelines. Often those who are in positions of influence in a local area will view those who are forward-thinking regarding group economics as a threat to the status quo. In some cases, they will even work against these visionary efforts and throw a monkey wrench in plans as they progress. Those who may eventually be supportive will usually take a wait-and-see approach, jumping aboard the proverbial train after it has already left the station.

Fear is one of the main underlying catalysts for the crab syndrome. There is fear of the unknown, fear that the small sliver of the economic pie that is available will vanish if one of us experiences a breakthrough, or fear that one person's success will make others appear inept.

Finally, mainstream media coverage will ultimately take a negative turn because media thrive on negativity—especially as it relates to black people. At first, they may cover an effort in a positive light. But they wait like vultures for something bad to happen and will immediately swoop in and provide ten times the amount of coverage if something goes wrong. Either out of habit or malicious intent, they are simply unable to expand their storylines for any significant amount of time beyond dysfunction, tragedy, and protest where black people are concerned.

Don't Throw Pearls Before Swine

The third mistake the Andersons made was spending much of their black year doing what the Bible describes in Matthew 7:6 as "throwing pearls before swine." Reading their cringe-worthy accounts of attempts to frequent poorly-run enterprises that should have been closed long before made me wonder why they persisted in supporting these businesses solely because they were owned by black people.

Their experience clearly validated the point that black ownership in and of itself is not enough. These are the types of businesses that feed the negative stereotype that black-owned enterprises are inferior.

Rather, it is better to do just the opposite and be selective about which black-owned firms are supported. The goal should be to support excellence (not to be confused with perfection) and above-average standards, those that defy stereotypes, because they have the greatest likelihood for success and job creation.

Operating at a level of excellence does not mean the business has to be located in the area's most expensive commercial district. It means the proprietors are responsive, dependable and proficient; deliver in a timely fashion; and communicate effectively. Good customer service and competitive pricing are also important.

Churches Experience Similar Challenges

Black churches that want to increase their support of black businesses can learn much from the Andersons' experience. Pastors and churches will encounter the same challenges as did the Chicago couple.

Dr. Sammie Holloway, pastor of Breath of Life Christian Center (www.bolcc.org) in Memphis, Tenn., has spent more than a decade putting the theory of group economics to the test. I met and interviewed Holloway and detailed his approach in my first book on group economics, *Why African Americans Can't Get Ahead: And How We Can Solve It With Group Economics*, published in 2008. The long-term results of his program highlight the challenges with implementing the concept of group economics within the black community, even with church involvement.

In the late 1990s Holloway spent nearly a full year teaching a series of sermons at his church on the truth about group economics from a biblical viewpoint. During a study of a familiar New Testament parable in Luke 19:11 – 27, known as the Parable of the Pounds, he received a revelation about wealth distribution. Verse 13, in particular, literally jumped off the page for Holloway as he was reading. "Occupy till I come" instructed Christians regarding what they should do until Jesus' return. In some versions of the Bible, the verse is more specific to commerce. The New International Version reads, "Put this money to work until I come back"; in the New American Standard Bible, it reads, "Do business with this until I come."

The Memphis minister believes it was Jesus' intent for members of the Body of Christ to practice this principle among themselves. "But, for the most part," says Holloway, "all other ethnicities in the Body of Christ choose to separate themselves from the African Diaspora. They only want to include the African Diaspora in commerce after all value has been added to a product from its very raw form. When it becomes a finished product, then [people of] the African Diaspora are welcomed at retail time," when the price of the product is at its highest.

At the heart of Holloway's approach is a simple principle: African Americans and others within the African Diaspora must begin to take the responsibility of practicing commerce from raw form to finished product relative to things that we consume. In doing so, we can provide jobs for our people, hope for children, education for our people, and everything else we need to function as a viable, respected group.

Holloway took a number of bold steps to put his vision into motion. In 2002, under his leadership, members of his church founded the Breath of Life Business Association (BOLBA), which is a separate entity under the auspices of the church that possesses its own non-profit status. Holloway encourages the members, as well as everyone else with whom he interacts, to purposely support the members of the BOLBA.

For the first few years of the Association's existence, a business was featured each week during Breath of Life's Sunday morning services. A representative of the business, selected by BOLBA, was presented to the church body, and Holloway provided the congregation with a brief overview of the person's business. In addition, Holloway held seminars at the church featuring speakers who were experts on the concept of group economics. The seminars were free to the church members and the public.

But Holloway moved his project beyond the theoretical stage to put it in action when Breath of Life erected a new worship center in 2005 and many of the subcontractors were members of the church. "These were the largest bids they had ever won," says Holloway, "and when they bid on large jobs around the country in the future, no general contractor could deny them with the excuse 'I'm sorry, but you don't have enough experience.'"

A residual effect of Breath of Life's commitment to hiring subcontractors within its own membership is that these same companies used primarily black craftsmen, thus circulating the dollars spent several times within the community. Holloway developed a formula for the vendor selection process, one that he still utilizes:

- First, can a member of the BOLBA provide the service or product? If not,
- Second, can a member of Breath of Life provide it? If not,
- Third, can a member of another black church provide it? If not,

- Fourth, can a member of a church within another ethnic group provide it? If not,

- Finally, we go to the larger community.

Holloway also reached out to members of the community whom some might consider to be unemployable. "It was in our plans to utilize some who have been in the criminal justice system and who are finding it difficult to get a second chance in the labor market," he says.

With his revelation, vision, and strategic plan in place, Holloway expected to get the ball rolling fairly quickly. But he was soon confronted with five almost insurmountable challenges:

- Getting black people to conspicuously use black businesses,

- Getting black people to stop judging black businesses *more critically* than businesses of other ethnic groups,

- Getting black entrepreneurs to see the need to join the Association for unified power,

- Getting new businesses to see the need for excellence at every level, and

- Getting new businesses to receive education and training to understand customer service, tax reporting, planning, budgeting, and all of the other essential elements of growing an enterprise.

When asked how the members of his church responded to his economic plan, Holloway said they responded slowly at first. "Initially, it seemed that they wanted to quickly execute the plan," he said, "but when they needed a product or service that [members of] the Business Association could provide, the members simply did not think about them."

"It was as if something blinded their minds when they were about to shop," he continued. "Finally, I realized that years of Jim Crow had completely suffused their minds to even the possibility of being serviced by a black business. So I began to remind them every week of the need to patronize black businesses."

Holloway experienced a common, pervasive problem. Too often African Americans conduct what amounts to a "death watch" of black-owned businesses. When a business opens, rather than immediately patronizing the entrepreneur and giving him/her encouragement—and much-needed dollars—to continue, black consumers will sit back and wait three to five years to see if the business is successful. The underlying expectation is that the business will fail, and because of the lack of customers and revenue, most of them do. There is then a sympathetic sigh that another one "bites the dust," when the public is partly to blame for its failure to spend money early and often with the business that has dared to take the risk of providing products and services to a usually underserved community.

Granted, many black business owners have expertise in a particular area and start a business in that field, but their knowledge of effective marketing techniques may be limited. In addition, many black businesses start with limited capital because the owners do not have the reservoir of well-heeled friends and family who can invest in their enterprise. This devastating trend of standing on the sidelines while black businesses are starving for customers must be reversed if wealth transfer is to decelerate.

Even with all of the energy Holloway put into his program, he found that his vision slowly languished a few years after it began. "It's like a spiritual warfare that we as a people have to break through," says Holloway with obvious disappointment.

"We had about a 30 percent success rate with the businesses that were part of the Association," says Holloway, whose church has a mortgage with a black-owned bank. The Memphis minister's vision was to include thousands of others for the benefit of the whole. In his view, as businesses flourished, the entire community, including his church, would flourish. But he found that most of the entrepreneurs did not share his overall vision and were operating purely in their own self-interest.

"The business owners did not want to hear about what it really took to get the job done," he said. Many of those who joined the Association "simply wanted to get customers from the church, not to service them in an excellent way," he added.

He also found difficulty in getting majority-black megachurches to adopt the principle of group economics. "Many are seemingly afraid to partner with other churches in working for the economic betterment of black people," he said. Holloway believes this apprehension stems from the desire of many megachurch pastors to reach beyond the black community and build multi-ethnic congregations. But Holloway asserts this is a short-sighted approach.

"We must not let a few Christians of other ethnicities joining predominantly black churches cause us to shut our eyes to the unique predicament of black people," he says. "If the non-blacks in our congregations are genuine, then they will acknowledge that black congregations must address this unique economic predicament of the African Diaspora. No other institution in the black community can fix it, and no institution in other ethnic groups is willing to fix it, including within the Body of Christ."

Holloway's approach moving forward is to work with other churches regardless of denomination. But he sees the lack of togetherness as a palpable deficit. "Group togetherness is what is going to lead to group economics," he said. "Churches will need to get together, not be ashamed to be black, and say they are going to do things to benefit black people."

CHAPTER 7

WHAT BLACK CHURCHES CAN DO

The first six chapters of this book were devoted to making the case that the black church is the central institution with the capacity to affect wealth transfer and retention. The remaining chapters concentrate on how the black church can, with the assistance of parishioners and entrepreneurs, play a larger role in group economics efforts and make wealth retention a reality.

What can black churches do now to begin moving wealth in a different direction so it directly benefits black communities? There are several action steps churches can take to increase the amount of wealth that is retained. Fortunately, most churches have already taken an important step through their community outreach programs.

Retaining Wealth Through Social Programs

The black church has traditionally been much more than just a religious institution among African Americans. It is also a social institution. Taking the principle to heart that "It takes a village to raise a child," thousands of black churches across America regularly sponsor programs such as food

81

pantries/soup kitchens, mentorship for at-risk youth, voter registration and education, drug treatment and counseling services, and outreach efforts to prisons and jails that fill needs unmet by the social safety net. Federal, state, and local government programs alone have never been sufficient enough to fill those needs.

Alfred Street Baptist Church in Alexandria, Va., for example, gives 2,000 low-income children backpacks and winter coats and provides health screenings for their families through its "Brother's Keeper" program.[76]

Fallbrook Church (www.fallbrookchurch.org) in Houston, Texas, sponsors an annual Community Bazaar where members donate gently used clothing, toys, and electronics which are provided free of charge to thousands of needy families in the greater Houston area. The 10,000-member church also hosts twice-yearly "Second Chance" programs, where attorneys and career counselors offer free advice for job seekers who cannot pass their background checks. Hundreds of potential job seekers take advantage of the programs.

Other churches offer Christian-based day care centers and educational academies for parents who would like their children to be nurtured in a wholesome atmosphere. Additional programs include housing for the elderly, computer training centers, and tutoring programs. These programs are more likely to be offered at churches with larger congregations.

The existence of social outreach programs appears to have a positive effect on church income. In a study titled *Black Church Giving,* researched by Vanderbilt University Professor Sandra L. Barnes, results showed that churches that sponsor more programs tend to receive greater contributions than those with fewer programs.[77]

More importantly, social outreach programs help fulfill the Great Commission—to spread the teachings of Jesus Christ to all the nations of the world; to feed the hungry; to offer comfort to the lost, hurting, and dispossessed; and to spread the Good News of salvation. Stymying the flow of wealth away from black communities and retaining more of the wealth to meet the human needs of the residents of those communities enhances the effectiveness of church-sponsored social outreach programs. Following are several methods churches can utilize to affect wealth retention.

Develop a Relationship With a Black-Owned Bank and/or Host a Banking/Finance Event

If there is a black-owned bank within the church's proximity (see list in Chapter 4), the pastor and/or church leaders can contact the bank president to discuss the possibility of opening an account and establishing a working relationship. Even if the church does not utilize a black-owned bank as its primary financial institution, an account could be opened to deposit reserve funds or as a secondary repository.

Black banks tend to be struck the hardest by economic downturns, primarily because the communities they serve suffer higher-than-average job losses and home foreclosure rates.[78] The result is a higher rate of bank closures and accounts for the small number of only 22 existing black-owned banks.

With this in mind, the church should not expect the bank to take any actions that are not within standard business practices, because to do so would be detrimental to both the bank and the church. But depending on the amount deposited, average monthly account balances, and credit history, the bank may be more receptive to approving loans, lines of credit, and mortgages. "Some customers get turned down by mainstream institutions for business loans and mortgages," says Michael A. Grant, president of the Washington, D.C.-based National Banker Association, "then come to black banks as a last resort—and get the loan."[79]

Hosting events where bank representatives can meet consumers and potentially provide financial education resources is another way churches can become involved in the wealth retention process. Jubilee Christian Church in Mattapan, Massachusetts, a majority-black neighborhood within the city of Boston, partnered with OneUnited Bank to host a banking event on September 10, 2016. The church's senior pastor, Matthew K. Thompson, describes the church as one of the largest black churches in New England.

Ironically, OneUnited loaned Thompson's father, whose tenure as pastor preceded the younger Thompson assuming the position as senior pastor, the funds for Jubilee to purchase one of its first buildings.[80] "He went to bank after bank after bank only to be told no," says Thompson about his father's search for bank financing for their first church building. "But Boston Bank of Commerce, now called OneUnited Bank, took a chance on my father and Jubilee."

During a summer trip to Paris with his wife, Mona, to celebrate their twentieth wedding anniversary, Thompson says he had an epiphany about Jubilee becoming a steward of his congregants' fiscal as well as spiritual health and, as a result, contacted OneUnited. Those discussions resulted in the creation of the #BankBlackBoston event, where new accounts were opened and information provided regarding financial literacy. OneUnited also held an event in Miami earlier the same year, where 550 new accounts were opened.[81]

Thompson, who opened an online savings account with OneUnited in advance of the event, believes the church's emphasis on economics and social justice will pay dividends for the next generation. "There is a collective potential that I believe the Lord wants us to understand and to realize, that we can do more together than we could ever do apart."

Thompson cited two scriptures to support his philosophy. The first is Proverbs 23:7: "As a man thinketh in his heart so is he." "We have to change our thinking," says Thompson. The second is Matthew 12:34: "Out of the abundance of your heart your mouth will speak." "It is not just about your thinking but then changing what you say and then changing your action. Your words have to precede your actions. You cannot think defeat and expect victory."

Increase Support of Black-Owned Businesses

There are several steps that black churches can take to jumpstart or increase their support of black-owned businesses—in both the short term and long term—thereby decreasing the transfer of wealth. Implementing one or more of these initiatives will also prolong the retention of wealth within black communities.

First, the pastor and church leaders can identify businesses within the congregation that may be able to provide needed services or products. This can be done by including a request for information in the church announcements or on the church website. Many churches have developed printed business directories or online directories that include their parishioners who own businesses. Utilizing member-run businesses will extend the amount of time that wealth is retained within the church body.

Second, to expand the pool of potential businesses to support, the church can identify black-owned businesses within its local community that it can support. Many cities have black business directories and there are several national online sources that are searchable by city, state, or zip code such as www.blackbusinesslist.com, www.beconomy.net, www.blackownedbiz.com, www.blackbusiness.org, and www.buyblack365.com.

Third, churches can permit businesses to bid on needed services or products, but they should also expect to pay market rates. Do not expect an automatic "church discount" or assume that the enterprise is giving the church a donation. If the service or product is provided as a donation, the arrangement should be clearly agreed upon in advance of the transaction. In addition, avoid requesting donations from community-based or black-owned companies the church, pastor, or church leaders have not supported in the past with their dollars.

If the church and its leaders can make an effort to contact the business owner when they are seeking support for activities and events, then they should be in the habit of thinking of the business and making a purchase when a product or service is needed. Allow the relationship to be a reciprocal one. After all, if the church and its leaders refuse to patronize these businesses, where will the companies obtain the funds to put into non-profit programs?

Fourth, once services are provided or products delivered, make payment in a timely manner. Unfortunately, some churches have a reputation of taking an inordinate amount of time to pay for services and, in some cases, do not pay for them at all. Business owners need paying customers rather than 90-day-old accounts receivable.

Also, consider forming a business owners' ministry for networking, training, and support. Having the ministry run by an entrepreneur who understands the needs of business owners is the best way to ensure that the effort stays alive and addresses relevant concerns.

Devin Robinson is founder of the Atlanta-based Urban Business Institute, which teaches black entrepreneurs how to establish and run successful businesses. Robinson has approached dozens of black churches about establishing entrepreneur programs as part of their ministries. The response has been mixed.

"I have worked with Donnie McClurkin's Perfecting Faith Church in Freeport, New York, and Pastor C. William Joyner Jr. at the Broadway Baptist Church in Augusta, Ga., both of whom provide information to their congregations about creating wealth and supporting community-based businesses," says Robinson about two of his consultations that have produced successful results. But sometimes pastors summarily reject the concept of teaching entrepreneurship to their congregants.

"I spoke to a black pastor at a black church in Alabama about hosting an entrepreneurship program at his church," describes Robinson, but the pastor said it would adversely affect his membership numbers and tithes and offerings. "The pastor told me in no uncertain terms that when people become successful, they stop coming to church and stop giving money to the church," Robinson continued. "That made me feel as though he didn't want to empower people legitimately because he wanted to hold them captive. Sometimes I feel that he and other pastors like him do not really want to free our people."

To be sure, the Alabama pastor Robinson describes is not universally representative. But his attitude and approach is not unique either, as there are a wide range of views regarding how pastors at black churches view business owners in terms of their impact on the church.

Finally, consider establishing a credit union to provide financial services for your church and its members. Information regarding starting a credit union is available online at www.mycreditunion.gov.

Think Outside the Box

Significant progress regarding stunting the flow of wealth transfer cannot be made by maintaining the status quo. Progress will require boldness, vision, and outside-the-box thinking.

A number of churches around the country are making wealth retention within black communities a priority and are developing a variety of methods to achieve that goal. In addition to identifying black-owned businesses, following are other projects that have been launched by black churches.

Development of Scholarship Funds

Hundreds of black churches have created scholarship funds that provide financial support to college students. The funds for these scholarships are raised in a variety of ways, including church-hosted banquets, golf tournaments, and direct scholarship fund drives.

In most cases, these scholarships are for amounts of $500 or less. However, in 2015 the First Church of God in Columbus, Ohio (www.1stchurch.net), partnered with the United Negro College Fund to provide a much larger scholarship award ranging from $2,500 to $10,000. Applicants were required to be high school seniors or enrolled college students and were required to submit a recommendation from a church member.

The Alfred Street Baptist Church (www.alfredstreet.org) in Alexandria, Va., the oldest and largest African-American congregation in the city, used a different approach by becoming a catalyst for scholarship awards by bringing together thousands of high school students and HBCU recruiters. The church began its annual HBCU College Festival in 2002. The Festival is held during Black History Month, and the 2016 event was the largest to date for the 7,000-member congregation, attracting over 3,000 students. Over 160 scholarships totaling $2.1 million were awarded to deserving students by the Historically Black Colleges and Universities represented at the Festival.[82]

Reviving Black Wall Street

The Dallas, Texas-based Friendship-West Baptist Church (www.friendshipwest.org) is reviving the spirit of the Black Wall Streets of the early 1900s by launching its own project, called "West Wall Street." The project was inspired by the Black Wall Street in the Greenwood district of Tulsa, Okla., that for nearly 20 years was a thriving business district. From the early 1900s until 1921 the number of black-owned businesses in Greenwood grew to more than 600, including a black-owned bus line, six real estate companies, wealthy oilmen, construction firms, and other entrepreneurs. Several black millionaires had businesses in Greenwood, six of whom owned private planes—at a time when there were only two airports in the entire state of Oklahoma.[83] A single dollar may have stayed in this tight-knit black community for almost a year before leaving.[84]

The district was burned to the ground by white rioters in 1921, and more than 300 black Tulsans were killed.[85] A television series based on Tulsa's Black Wall Street is being produced by pop artist John Legend for the WGN Network, which could debut in 2018 if picked up as a series.[86]

Friendship-West's primary goal in launching West Wall Street is to economically empower the southern sector of Dallas and black businesses. According to the mission statement posted on its website, Friendship-West believes in "cooperative economics" and the "need for businesses to work together and share resources much like the African Nations and civilizations did prior to slavery."

The church's first West Wall Street (www.friendshipwest.org/west-wall-street.html) event was held in April 2016, with another one planned for November. The project includes the launch of the church's own business directory and the creation of a network of black businesses in the Dallas area.[87] Initiatives similar to West Wall Street can be duplicated and developed by black churches across the United States.

Pastors Are Not Instant Proprietors, and Ministers Are Not Instant Merchants

Black churches have a long history of launching ancillary non-profit entities that complement their community outreach efforts. The most common are day care centers, schools, drug treatment centers, and homes for the elderly. In general, these entities are largely successful and, if properly managed, can remain in operation and serve the local community for decades.

When black churches venture into the realm of for-profit enterprises, such as restaurants, beauty salons, coffee shops and banks, they are much less likely to succeed. One reason is pastors do not instantly become top-notch proprietors when a church-run business is opened. It was already mentioned in Chapter 2 that the majority of black pastors do not possess earned bachelor's degrees, and among those who do, their studies are largely limited to ministry, religion or humanities. Few have backgrounds or college degrees in business or economics, nor do they have experience running a business enterprise.

One example of less than successful church-run enterprises occurred at a Houston megachurch that opened a restaurant and beauty salon on its premises in the 1990s. Within two years, both enterprises were closed due to customer complaints of subpar customer service, including long wait times for service. The church opened a Christian academy in the 2000s that included grades kindergarten through sixth. The academy closed within five years due to financial shortfalls.

An anointing in Christian ministry does not automatically translate into an understanding of what is required to make a business successful. The former is a divine calling that requires faith, sacrifice, and, if one adheres to principles exhibited by Jesus Christ, an emphasis on the less fortunate. The latter, on the other hand, requires a focus on profitability. The decisions required to earn a profit can sometimes be tough—even draconian by some standards.

Even for those pastors who do have a business background, like Dr. Bill Winston of Chicago's Living Word Christian Center, who spent several years as a regional manager for IBM, results can be mixed, as described in Chapter 6. There are hundreds of examples of churches that attempted to launch for-profit entities only to have them fail within a short period of time.

A second reason church-run businesses have a less-than-favorable success rate is that the market forces at work in the for-profit business environment do not easily align with many biblical principles. To succeed, a business must have an experienced management team, a sound financial plan, a solid marketing strategy, and a competitive advantage. A business must service customers who can pay, not provide those services to those who need them most but happen to be cash-poor. To do otherwise is to invite disaster.

Churches have found that even members of their congregations require a high level of service and are not willing to tolerate the long waits and poor customer service often found at church-run establishments. The members will likely give the church-run business a chance but will eventually move on if the service is not up to par.

Although members of a congregation may believe in their pastor's calling, he or she does not suddenly become a jack of all trades. Their skills as spiritual leaders do not automatically translate into financial prowess or increase their business acumen. For a business to succeed, including a church-run business, it must have a sound business plan, have experienced management, and earn enough profits to sustain itself. With this in mind, churches should proceed with caution, making sure all i's are dotted and all t's are crossed before committing the church's resources to a for-profit endeavor.

CHAPTER 8

WHAT PARISHIONERS CAN DO

Parishioners are consumers, and consumers have power—often more than they realize. When parishioners are motivated to effect change, positive results can occur very quickly. That is what is required to begin reversing the wealth transfer back to black communities.

The first step is to believe that wealth retention is possible. This is the most difficult and most important step of all, but once this hurdle is crossed, results will be immediate and long-lasting. Our collective belief in our ability to achieve success as a group has been severely hampered by our history of slavery and discrimination. Coupled with the daily negative images of African Americans perpetuated by the media, this one-two punch has devastated our individual and collective psyches.

We must literally reprogram our minds with positive affirmations or confessions. Here is one based upon the biblical principles of Philippians 4:13: "I can do all things, including wealth transfer, through Christ who strengthens me." For those African Americans who may not be Christian or practice any particular religion, here is another: "There is nothing that I cannot achieve, including wealth transfer, if I put my mind to it."

Here is still another: "I will not allow the inequities of lack and poverty suffered by previous generations to be passed on to my children. I will spend my dollars where they most benefit me and my community."

Repeated daily, these affirmations will fortify one's belief system and simultaneously neutralize some of the negativity we are exposed to regarding group success. And success is indeed possible as exemplified by the push to support black banks that occurred in the summer of 2016.

#BankBlack Movement

Following several years of incidents where white police officers were exonerated after shooting and killing either unarmed or restrained black men, the anger within the black community seemed to culminate into, among other things, a movement to support black-owned banks. The movement appears to have been sparked by two occurrences: One was a chain of text messages that originated at Howard University and encouraged recipients to open an account at a black bank and to forward the text message to several of their friends. The text message quickly spread throughout the country, and the response was swift.

The second was a July 8 interview with hip-hop artist Killer Mike on Atlanta's Hot 97 radio station during which he encouraged blacks in the city to put their money to work in response to police shootings and other systemic injustices by depositing money in the local Citizen's Trust bank or any black-owned bank. Then a Greek organization website called Watch the Yard posted an article on July 9, 2016, that listed black-owned banks and credit unions and encouraged members of black fraternities and sororities to support these institutions.[88]

Within a few days, Atlanta's Citizens Trust Bank, founded in 1921, experienced more than 8,000 people opening new accounts within a five-day period.[89] The influx of new deposits caught the attention of bank CEO Cynthia N. Day, who used Twitter to send a public thank you message to Killer Mike on July 8, for his call-to-action. "Together, we can change the conversation," she wrote in her tweet.[90]

Unity National Bank in Houston also experienced an influx of new customers opening accounts, including a group of more than a dozen local rappers. John Scroggins, president and CEO of Unity, said more than 300 customers opened new accounts at their two locations within 72 hours. "I think the primary reason was the new consciousness of the African-American community that they want to do business with African-American-owned enterprises and businesses," he said in an interview with *Fox News* on July 13, 2016. "I think that's the main focus."

The ripple effects continued when, a few days later, Boston's black-owned OneUnited Bank also experienced a rush in new deposits. OneUnited's president and chief operating officer Teri Williams said both its website traffic and deposit applications increased ten-fold during the same time period. "We have had people line up at our bank to open up accounts," said Williams. OneUnited is the nation's largest black-owned bank with $650 million in assets, and has additional locations in Miami and Los Angeles.[91]

North Carolina's Mechanics & Farmers Bank, the nation's oldest black-owned bank, which has been in business since 1907, signed up $1.25 million in new accounts in five days, according to bank representative Jasmine Parker. "It's good to see these dollars being recycled back into the community," she said.[92]

Similar results were experienced by the Illinois Federal Savings and Loan in Chicago, which had $4 million in new deposits within a one-week period;[93] by New York City's Carver Federal Savings Bank, which collected $2.4 million in new deposits; and Washington, D.C.'s Industrial Bank, where 1,500 new accounts were opened during the month of July alone, an amount that usually occurred over a six-month period.[94] [95]

According to Michael Grant, president of the Washington, D.C.-based National Bankers Association, which promotes minority-owned financial institutions, CEOs of black-owned banks said the activity was not limited to only a few banks. "It's not just happening in one location—it's happening to banks around the country," said Grant in a *USA Today* interview.[96] "These [police] killings released a sense of hopelessness and frustration, and this volcanic eruption happened for us to do something positive, to put our energies into something that can help solve problems," he added in a separate interview.[97]

Black banks may be buoyed by the #BankBlack movement, but hashtag efforts tend to be short-lived as the attention span of the American public moves on to the next issue that captures its imagination. Some financial observers, however, are hopeful. "The idea of opening up an account at a black-owned bank is the best baby step in creating a financial statement of black political solidarity while simultaneously building personal wealth for you and your family," wrote Kara I. Stevens in an *Ebony* magazine article on August 12, 2016. "Consider sharing articles about black wealth or organizing visits to black banks to make sure that this movement outlives its hashtag's popularity," she added.[98]

A Sustained Effort Is Crucial

In order to be effective, efforts to support black institutions and businesses must be a sustained effort, not simply a response to a crisis. Too often, the motivation is to send a message to the larger society, not necessarily based on the principle of supporting and building black-owned institutions. Once the crisis ends and the associated energy dissipates, economic efforts like this tend to fizzle. Group economics must become a habit; it must be a way of life and more than simply a reactionary response.

Righteous indignation and anger alone will not solve this problem. We cannot depend on boycotts, marches, or demonstrations to try to force others to be benevolent. Years of continuous support of black-owned institutions are required for substantial change to occur. But history has not yet shown that a sustained effort can be realized once the crisis is over.

Even one of the most successful economic protests in U.S. history, the Montgomery Bus Boycott of 1955, saw its resultant multi-car transportation network disappear once the boycott ended. In 1955 Rosa Parks' refusal to give up her bus seat to a white man inspired Montgomery, Alabama's 48,000 Negro residents to launch a citywide bus boycott. Parks' role in the boycott is well documented, but the economic impact of the boycott has received much less historical attention.

Under the leadership of Dr. Martin Luther King Jr., this movement was immediately 90 percent effective and continued for an extraordinary 381 days, constituting the first large-scale and enduring modern protest for Negro rights and an example of the power of group economics.[99] The car pool system alone, involving more than 200 cars and 40 regular pickup points, was an organizational wonder.[100]

Although the boycott succeeded in forcing the bus company to allow black riders to sit wherever they wanted, its fatal flaw was its narrow objective. The boycott's goal was to go from sitting in the back of the bus to the front of the bus, side by side with white people. There was no goal of ownership or wealth creation, which could have been easily achieved had the boycott been turned into a more expansive economic movement.

In fact, since leaders of the movement had purchased a fleet of station wagons for use during the boycott, the next logical step—had they been group economics-minded— would have been to use these vehicles to create an alternative transportation system where discrimination would no longer be an issue. Sadly, the leaders of that time did not have a vision of economic independence for African Americans. But perhaps this represented a bridge too far in terms of their current conditions under the stranglehold of racial apartheid.

Even more unfortunate is that more than 60 years later, a visionary approach is still seemingly light-years away. Righteous indignation is a good starting point, but economic efforts must move from the realm of a purely emotional reaction to an intellectual understanding that our long-term survival depends upon collective wealth creation. These efforts must move from theory to reality.

"It [is] easy to get people stirred up about the potential for large-scale economic empowerment, recycling our wealth, enhancing our neighborhoods, demanding more respect from big business for our consumer dollars, and reclaiming our community from folks who take our money and treat us with disrespect," writes Maggie Anderson in her book, *Our Black Year*. "It [is] much harder to inspire excitement about actually going into poor black communities and patronizing struggling businesses."[101]

But one does not have to take a trek into impoverished communities in order to support black-owned companies. For many decades, black-owned businesses have moved beyond poverty-stricken areas and are now located in bustling downtown districts and growing suburbs. These companies provide income for black families and employ black teenagers, sometimes through high school cooperative programs, where students learn job skills, earn an income, and receive classroom credit.

Based on the Andersons' year-long experience, the Kellogg Business School conducted a study that revealed only 2 to 3 percent of the $1.2 trillion earned annually among black consumers stays within the black community. "But the study also showed that if middle class consumers could increase that number to just 10 percent, we would create over 1 million new jobs," said Anderson. "No government programs, no corporate donations, just us."

Think About Your *Dollars* Before Spending Them

Much of an individual's disposable income is usually spent within their community or city. In your daily activities where spending money is involved, particularly discretionary spending for personal items, entertainment, clothing, insurance, etc., ask yourself this question: Is there a reputable African-American-owned business from which I can purchase this product or service?

The answer may often be "no" since, as stated in Chapter 6, there is a dearth of black-owned businesses that provide essential services, such as groceries, clothing, gasoline, and personal care items. In many cases, it will be virtually impossible to locate a black-owned firm in your area that provides these items at all, let alone at competitive prices. But for those that do exist, they will need customers who patronize them on a regular basis in order to survive. You can also expand your search by patronizing black-owned businesses that have an Internet presence and are located in different parts of the country. Occasionally frequenting the black business is not enough.

Identify and develop a list of African-American businesses you will patronize during the coming year. To expand your list, elicit input from friends and family. Include addresses, phone numbers, websites, and email addresses to make your list comprehensive. Include the companies in your cell phone's contact list for easy access.

For those businesses you cannot personally patronize, try to refer others to them. For example, you may be aware of a business that provides catering services that you may not presently need. However, you may have a friend or colleague that needs catering for an upcoming event, and you could make a referral.

Refer Reputable Businesses to the Church

For businesses, the best marketing is word-of-mouth or a referral by a satisfied customer. If parishioners are familiar with reputable black-owned businesses that provide services the church already uses or may need in the future, they can provide a referral to the pastor or someone in church leadership. A referral will ease the way for an entrepreneur to present a bid for services he or she offers. It is important that entrepreneurs who are referred by church members follow through with excellence in their performance, which will make it easier for other businesses to get a foot in the door.

Avoid Unreasonable Expectations of Black-Owned Enterprises

Too often when patronizing black-owned businesses, the consumer approaches the business transaction with the expectation that things will go wrong. If we expect disaster, bad things will tend to occur. Comments from online articles on topics related to black businesses and banks are instructive regarding the unreasonable expectations and demands some black consumers place on black enterprises.

For example, in an online discussion regarding depositing money in black banks, one commenter questioned the interest rate on savings accounts at black banks, suggesting that they should be willing to pay 5 percent or more in interest. To do so is not only unrealistic but also would be detrimental for the bank since the average interest rate on savings accounts nationwide has been about 0.06 percent for the past several years. Expecting black banks to pay interest rates 80 times above the norm is not only a disastrous business policy; it's just plain ridiculous.

Teri Williams, president of the black-owned bank OneUnited, expressed some frustration with the questions bank representatives are asked by some potential, but skeptical, black customers. "They ask us if the bank is really black-owned, whether or not we are FDIC-insured, and if we offer the same services as large banks," said Williams. They "believe that their [white-owned business'] ice is colder," she added, referencing the centuries-old adage that some black people embrace. "We have accepted a lot of the negativity that is talked about in our community. But we have to start trusting each other and doing business with each other."

Also, it is unreasonable to compare any black-owned enterprise to its billion-dollar competitor. For example, do not expect a local retailer to be able to match Wal-Mart's prices. Behemoths like Wal-Mart and Target are able to sell items at less expensive prices than much smaller companies as a result of three primary retail principles:

- **Volume purchasing.** A small company that buys 100 units of a product is going to pay considerably more per unit than a multinational company that purchases 1 million units of the same item. The price differential may be considerable; for example, the small company could pay $1.00 per unit versus 25 cents per unit for Wal-Mart. The small company may try to sell the item for $2.00, thus doubling its money. By comparison, Wal-Mart can sell the item for 50 cents, also doubling its money but selling it to the consumer at a much lower price. If the small company tries to match Wal-Mart's price, it will lose money on every sale and quickly go out of business. Of course, the consumer wants to pay the least amount but should understand the economics behind why the small retailer cannot match what Wal-Mart charges.

- **Economies of scale.** A multinational company with hundreds of locations can operate each location more cheaply than a small company with one location. That is because the larger company can spread some of its costs among all of the stores, thus lowering the costs per store. This economic principle of being able to spread costs over a broad number of locations is known as economies of scale.

- **Loss leader.** Previously referred to in Chapter 6, a loss leader is an item a retailer will use as an inducement to get customers into its stores. This item is usually sold at cost, or at a loss, to get foot traffic in the store. These customers will then, presumably, purchase other items at regular or higher profit margins. The "loss leader" tactic is used by large retailers that sell thousands of items and is not generally available to the small retailer with a limited inventory and fewer locations.

In general, a small business will not be able to compete with a billion-dollar, multinational company on the basis of price or convenience. However, small businesses offer the advantages of personalized service, specialty product lines, and ready access to top management. Saving money matters, and consumers should understandably budget their dollars strategically. But consumers, when making purchasing decisions, should also consider the strengths that a small company can offer.

Don't Overreact When Problems Arise

In business, it is inevitable that challenges will occur from time to time. Negative situations that customers experience should be kept at a minimum, but the fact that the problem exists is not the issue; rather, the manner in which the problem is resolved is what measures the effectiveness and integrity of the entrepreneur.

As a customer, do not overreact when the problem occurs. *In other words, don't go off!* Do not immediately put the business on blast via social media, threaten to tell everyone you know, or report the company to the Better Business Bureau, the State Attorney General's Office or the President of the United States. These reactions are counterproductive, empty threats and cannot solve your problem.

Discuss Problems Directly With the Owner

Business owners are not perfect; they are human and make mistakes. Because of the long hours they work, they are often overwhelmed. Give the entrepreneur the benefit of the doubt. When you experience a challenge with a business transaction, speak with the manager or owner of the company directly, and give him or her an opportunity to rectify the error. Make sure you are speaking with the person who can actually make a decision.

Give the entrepreneur sufficient time and the opportunity to correct the mistake. Be courteous, and say thank you when he or she resolves the dispute. Admit when you, the consumer, are wrong! Once the error is corrected give him or her another opportunity, and patronize the business again and again.

There is anecdotal evidence that we tend to be much tougher with our criticism of black-owned businesses than we are of other businesses. There are many examples of people from other cultures being unfriendly or rude to us when we make purchases in their stores. Yet we continue to spend money with them over and over again. Meanwhile, these same businesses rarely hire anyone from our communities, and they take the profits they make from these transactions back to their own neighborhoods, where they improve their housing and community services. Your commitment to the group economics principle will ensure that dollars circulate in our communities multiple times rather than leaving as soon as you receive your paycheck.

Of course, if a business owner engages in unscrupulous, unethical, or illegal practices, he or she obviously should not be patronized under any circumstances, no matter his or her ethnicity. The existence and proliferation of crooked businesses only damages the progress of group economics and makes it more difficult for legitimate businesses to become stronger and to expand.

Don't Allow One Bad Experience to Deter You

Cathy Hughes, founder of Radio One and TV One, alluded to a typical excuse many African Americans give for not patronizing their own businesses. "I tried doing business with a black company, but…" is a common statement, implying that the experience was not error-free.

"You don't stop doing business with white companies because one of them disappointed you," said Hughes in comments she made as a panelist at the 2007 State of the Black Union program held at Hampton University. Although she made her comments several years ago, Hughes' words were never more relevant than they are today. "We need to make a commitment to patronize our own businesses, no matter what," she concluded.

In other words, the principle of practicing group economics should be a strong motivator that cannot be derailed by one or two unpleasant experiences. Its practice must be deliberate, purposeful, and persistent. It is not a practice that is done for one day, on a designated holiday or weekend, when you receive a viral text message, or when the spirit moves. It is a way of life—a determination to, without procrastinating or making excuses, identify credible businesses that one can patronize and do so as often as possible.

When a business owner does a good job, give him or her encouragement and, more importantly, more business and referrals. An entrepreneur works long hours and makes many sacrifices to pursue the dream of economic independence. They may go without vacations or days off for years before their business becomes profitable. They fail more often than they succeed, but they keep on trying. And the existence of thousands of successful businesses is a key element of a winning group economics strategy.

Patronize Businesses Early and Often

Do not wait to see if a black-owned business is successful first before you decide to support it. When a business opens, it needs your patronage from day one and your continued support in the weeks and months that follow. It can only be successful if *you* support it and encourage others to do so. Do not procrastinate and assume others will support it. Do not make the excuse that it is too hard or too time-consuming. The hope and prosperity of future generations is depending on *you*.

In *Our Black Year*, Chicago group economics activist Maggie Anderson voiced her ultimate frustration with black consumers who somehow think patronizing black businesses once in their lifetimes qualifies as true support. Anderson described them this way:

> The Black folks who want credit for trying to buy Black once, ten years ago, and having an unsatisfactory experience, which leads them to dismiss the entire race as being incompetent business people.[102]

Teach the Principles of Group Economics and Wealth Transfer to Your Children

Take your children with you when you patronize an African-American business and explain to them the importance of circulating dollars within our own community. If they see you doing this on a regular basis, it will become part of their routine as they mature and become adults.

The principle of group economics can take root and be passed on from generation to generation if you start now with your children. The Bible says it best:

> Train up a child in the way he should go, and when he grows old, he will not depart from it. (Proverbs 22:6)

Celebrate Excellence and Avoid Negativity

With the above in mind, when you have a positive experience with an African-American business owner, be sure to verbalize your appreciation by celebrating excellence. Too often—in fact, in the vast majority of instances—when a black person details their experience utilizing a black-owned firm it is to describe a negative experience. Rarely does a black person start a sentence with "I went to a black-owned company" and the rest of the sentence has anything good to say about what occurred. That pattern needs to be reversed.

Rather than talk ad nauseum about how bad some black businesses are we should celebrate the ones that are good. If you have a *good* experience at a black-owned business, spread the word. Create a post on social media touting your positive experience and including a link to the company's website, Facebook page, or Instagram page. Allow the cheers to drown out the boos.

Keep the Big Picture in Mind

Your support of African-American businesses has long-term and far-reaching implications. There is much at stake for current and future generations. Many within the current generation appear to be without hope and in a downward spiral of despair. Their personal circumstances, lack of quality education, and poor job prospects lead many to resort to lives of crime, ultimately leading to early deaths or decades behind bars. Transferring the wealth back to black communities can help some of these young people see a light at the end of the tunnel. Each time you spend your dollars, be confident that you are retaining or creating jobs for many in the African-American community.

CHAPTER 9

WHAT ENTREPRENEURS CAN DO

Let's face it: In general, black-owned businesses do not have a favorable reputation. Overall, they are viewed negatively by black consumers. This negative reputation must be reversed if wealth retention is to be fully realized. Many of these wounds are self-inflicted ones. Black entrepreneurs must raise their performance standards, not only when doing business with churches but in general. Of course, this does not apply to all businesses as there are many black entrepreneurs for whom excellence in performance is an absolute necessity. However, for far too many, the attitude is nonchalant.

Black entrepreneurs must realize they are operating in a competitive environment where churches and consumers have numerous options when selecting vendors. They may consider the fact that they have a black-owned firm to be an advantage when approaching a black church. In reality, because of the overall negative reputation of black-owned companies, even those who operate with a high standard may have difficulty. As a result, all businesses should make it an objective to raise their image and performance levels. Do not expect churches to settle for subpar quality and shoddy service based on misplaced ethnic pride. Competitive pricing should be commensurate with the quality and services offered.

Pastors who were interviewed for this book indicated five major areas of concern when utilizing African-American businesses. The one cited repeatedly was the quality of customer service.

Subpar Customer Service

The complaint most often lodged when asked about their encounters with African-American-owned businesses was the lack of customer service. A positive, pleasant attitude is a basic part of business success, and, too often, African-American business establishments neglect this small detail. A smile and a pleasant attitude cost nothing but reap tremendous future rewards.

Other manifestations of poor customer service include:

- Failure to answer phones, return calls, or respond to emails in a timely manner;
- Failure to submit bids and paperwork in a timely manner;
- Failure to create a professional work environment or one that is aesthetically appealing; and

- Failure to complete jobs or deliver products on time.

"Most of my negative experiences with black businesses have been due to a lack of customer service," says Dr. Timothy Boddie of the Progressive National Convention. "I still try to give black businesses the benefit of the doubt, but that's an area where we could use a lot of work."

Boddie added that in the numerous environments where he has worked as a professional—including the Convention, as the pastor of two churches, and as a faculty member on HBCU campuses—he has repeatedly been confronted with this issue. "It's an area that really turns off a lot of middle-class and upper-middle-class black people, and it's unfortunate."

Accessibility is also very important for a small business that is trying to grow. If possible, businesses should have a live person answering the phone during normal business hours. If this is not possible, be sure to respond to voice mail messages within 24 hours. Large, multi-billion dollar corporations have the luxury of keeping customers on hold for extended periods with digital voice prompts. Small businesses do not.

High Prices

Pricing and quality are also concerns for some pastors who have utilized black-owned firms. "Unfortunately, whenever you mention church, people have an idea that there's a lot of money to be made, and sometimes they overcharge us," says Rev. Henry Prosper of Westfield Community Baptist Church in Houston. "Black enterprises have to be careful with their rates and make sure their prices are competitive. As a steward of the church's money, I have an obligation to get the lowest rates I can get with the best quality I can get."

Substandard Quality

Prosper says the high prices and low quality are a Catch-22 for him when considering black vendors. "Unfortunately, sometimes black-owned businesses are more expensive with lower quality. We have to improve our quality."

"Sometimes people don't take the church seriously," Prosper continued. "I do like to keep our money circulating in the community. But the problem I run into over and over again—even with church members who have businesses or who want to be employed by the church—is that because it's the church, they don't take the work as seriously as they would if it was a white church."

Defy Stereotypes

Businesses should strive to go against the grain—defy the stereotypes that taint all black-owned companies—by over-performing rather than underperforming. There is an old adage among black people that when competing in corporate America, we have to be twice as good as other employees to receive the recognition we deserve. Unfortunately, due to the negative reputation that exists for black businesses, black entrepreneurs must do the same. If a critical mass is reached that begins to defy those stereotypes, they will eventually fade away.

"We need to get back to the days when we knew the value of our work and took pride in what we did," says Pastor Prosper. "For anything we do—whether it's volunteering or working at the church—we have to get back to a good work ethic."

Embrace Technology

The world has evolved to a society where communication is done largely via the Internet, social media, and mobile devices. Entrepreneurs must embrace this new world with arms wide open and become involved at whatever level their resources will allow.

At a minimum, if your company does not currently have a website, create a simple one with the basics about your business. Make sure the information is spelled correctly and is accurate, especially your business name, address, and phone number. (This may appear to be obvious, but I have visited dozens of websites where the basic information was misspelled, the address was incorrect, or the listed phone number was disconnected.)

Your company should also have an active presence on social media (e.g., Facebook, Twitter, and/or Instagram) since individuals seeking products and services will often explore options there first. The absence or presence of a significant number of fans and followers will reflect your company's customer base and whether or not you are actively engaged in commerce. It may be worthwhile to promote your business using paid advertising on Facebook and/or Instagram to build your base of followers since visitors to your social media pages check those numbers and draw assumptions on that basis.

Also, respond to email inquiries within 24 hours. People are much more likely to do business with you if you can be reached easily and are accessible.

Black-Owned Banks Must Meet Even Higher Standards

Black-owned banks should embrace all of the suggestions already cited in this chapter. But as depositories of the people's funds, they must meet an even higher standard. According to banking experts, black banks have been slow to adopt the technology that has become ubiquitous with banking today.[103] Online banking and bill payment, as well as mobile banking, are no longer luxuries but necessities for banks that want to remain competitive.

Finally, and more importantly, as African Americans move money *en masse* to black-owned banks, bank executives should take this opportunity to tighten their proverbial ships and improve efficiency. As millions of dollars come into their coffers as a result of the #BankBlack movement, investments in experienced personnel, technology, and infrastructure—not exorbitant salary increases for bank owners and executives—should be priorities. Bank executives should show the people the same respect that the people have shown them.

CHAPTER 10

WHAT THE FUTURE COULD LOOK LIKE

Change always starts with a few people and grows from there. It builds like a snowball rolling down a hill and picks up momentum along the way. The same will be true among black churches, parishioners, and community leaders who begin to take wealth retention seriously. It will start with a few, and hopefully, as more pastors become aware of its importance, wealth will be retained, and black communities will begin to thrive.

The first thing that black Christians must do is renew our minds. As Romans 12:2 (NKJV) reads: "And do not be conformed to this world, but be transformed by the renewing of your mind, that you may prove what is that good and acceptable and perfect will of God."

Conforming to this world means that we continue to adopt all of the negative stereotypes about black-owned enterprises and wealth retention—that we continue to repeat negative statements and believe any efforts to change are defeated before they have begun. Renewing our minds means

123

that we start—right now, today, not next week or next month or next year—to think differently and speak differently.

Thousands of us will need to start thinking differently and believing differently if wealth transfer is to be reversed. The Bible, of course, is a sound source for a God-centered approach as well as understanding the importance of humility and integrity in dealing with others. Reading books that explain economics, the movement of money, and how it affects communities would be helpful. Motivational books can help us maintain a positive outlook even when so much of the news and public banter are decidedly negative. Philippians 4:8 (NKJV) provides us with the proper approach:

> Finally, brethren, whatever things are true, whatever things are noble, whatever things are just, whatever things are pure, whatever things are lovely, whatever things are of good report, if there is any virtue and if there is anything praiseworthy—meditate (or think) on these things.

Another thing black Christians will have to do in the short run is to stop waiting on God to take care of this problem. Black Christians seem to spend a lot of time waiting: waiting on God, waiting on Jesus' second coming, waiting on the Rapture, waiting on the afterlife, or waiting on some benevolent white person to deliver us from our current situation.

"Within the black church, too many of us have the attitude that 'God is going to take care of it,'" says Devin Robinson, founder of the Urban Business Institute. "What Christians need is knowledge so they can have the confidence to put their faith to work. If we did, the impact we could have within just one week would be powerful."

As was the case with the end of slavery and the fight for civil rights in the 1960s, God was waiting on us to take matters into our own hands. Once enough of us had made up our minds, with His help, we were able to do great things. Wealth retention will not occur unless we take action. We must begin to see our future in our own hands, using our God-given ability to chart a destiny that is not contingent upon what any other group does. Taking some of the action steps included in Chapters 7, 8, and 9 is a good start.

Wealth retention will require that skilled individuals who have expertise in an area or discipline consider and pursue starting and building a business. Chapter 5 detailed a variety of services and products that churches regularly utilize, and these could be businesses to consider since a demand has already been identified.

A business can be started on a part-time basis first and, once it is profitable enough to sustain an income for you and your family, can be turned into a full-time endeavor. At the very least, you can provide long-term security for yourself and members of your family. You can also create an asset you can leave to your children as well as create jobs for others.

Finally, although we should raise our expectations, they should also be tempered with realism. The wealth transfer that occurs every Monday morning as churches make their deposits in banks not owned or controlled by African Americans has occurred for decades and will not change overnight. Neither will the outflow of wealth via the utilization of non-African American-owned vendors.

But even a small shift would make a significant difference. As detailed in this book's Introduction and asserted by OneUnited Bank president Teri Williams, if the amount of income that is retained within black communities grows from its current 2 percent to 10 percent, one million new jobs could be created in our communities. That would be an absolute miracle!

Moreover, families can get involved. If 1,000 black families in every major city in America made a commitment to spend at least $2,000 annually with black-owned businesses, that equals an extra $2 million that could result in the creation of dozens of new jobs. If the amount increases each year, many more future jobs will be created in our communities, the level of hope and optimism will increase, and the next generation will have much to look forward to.

Even if the amount spent is smaller, the important thing is to get started. We all have to start somewhere. The involvement of every person and every aspect of the African-American community is the only way for the principles of wealth retention and group economics to take root and to create a new reality.

Gwen Richardson

ACKNOWLEDGEMENTS

No author can complete a book project without the assistance of others. First, I would like to thank God for bestowing upon me the gift of writing and an analytical mind. I have always tried to use my gifts with integrity and in the spirit of sharing knowledge with others and will continue to do so.

Next I would like to thank my husband, Willie A. Richardson, for his total and complete support during our now 24 years of marriage. I am fortunate to have a life partner who holds nothing back and understands and accepts me for who I am. Our daughter, Sylvia, is presently in her junior year in college and has always been a source of joy and pride.

I would also like to thank all of the pastors who agreed to be interviewed for this book. They each took time out of their busy schedules to provide input on this important subject, and their direct knowledge was crucial. They also represented a cross-section geographically and denominationally.

The following pastors were interviewed for *Weekend Wealth Transfer*: Dr. Michael Armstrong, senior pastor of Colesville United Methodist Church in Silver Spring, Md.; Dr. Timothy Boddie, General Secretary and Chief Operating Officer for the Progressive National Baptist Convention, headquartered in Washington, D.C., and former pastor of Friendship Baptist Church in Atlanta, Ga.; Rev. Sammie Holloway, senior pastor of Breath of Life Christian Center in Memphis, Tenn.; Rev. Kevin Wayne Johnson, senior pastor of Accokeek First Church of God in Accokeek, Md.; Rev. Henry Prosper, senior pastor of Westfield Community Baptist Church in Houston, Tex.,; and Rev. Dean Rodgers, senior pastor of the Salvation and Praise Worship Center in Hampton, Va.

Devin Robinson, founder of the Atlanta-based Urban Business Institute, was also interviewed. Robinson works closely with churches to help them establish entrepreneurship programs and his insights were invaluable.

I would like to thank two of my Facebook friends, Shay Olivarria and Karen Cecile Wallace, for their assistance with this book. Shay is a Los Angeles-based financial education speaker and author at Bigger Than Your Block who provided an Excel spreadsheet of minority-controlled federal credit unions. This list was the foundation for the comprehensive list of black-owned, faith-based credit unions listed in this book in Chapter 4. Karen is a Chicago-based attorney who made me aware of the economic program championed by Friendship-West Baptist Church in Dallas, Texas. I have never met Shay or Karen face-to-face, but communicate with them regularly via social media.

Finally, I would like to thank all who have read this or any of my eight published books. I believe this book, in particular, is one of my most important works. As I continue to write on contemporary topics of importance, I appreciate your continued support and feedback. I can be reached via email at gwenrichardson123@gmail.com.

Gwen Richardson

ABOUT THE AUTHOR

Gwen Richardson has been a writer and editor for more than 20 years. Her commentaries have appeared in several daily newspapers, including *USA Today, Houston Chronicle, Detroit Free Press, Dallas Morning News* and *Philadelphia Inquirer.*

A long-time entrepreneur and a graduate of Georgetown University, Ms. Richardson currently resides in Houston, Texas. She has been twice nominated for an NAACP Image Award for Outstanding Literary Work. This is her eighth published book.

Visit the author's website for information about other published books: www.gwenrichardson.com.

Communication via email is welcome. Email the author at gwenrichardson123@gmail.com.

Gwen Richardson

ENDNOTES

[1] "Does a dollar spent in the Black community really stay for only six hours?" Feb. 8, 2016, *The Louisiana Weekly*, www.louisianaweekly.com, Accessed August 31, 2016.

[2] Ann Brown, "OneUnited Bank's President Teri Williams Explains Why It's Smart to Bank Black—Just Like Solange," July 15, 2016, MadameNoire, www.madamenoire.com, Accessed July 16, 2016.

[3] "Underground Railroad: The William Still Story," Public Broadcasting Service, www.pbs.org, Accessed June 20, 2016.

[4] *PowerNomics*, Dr. Claud Anderson, PowerNomics Corporation of America, 2001, p. 223.

[5] Pew Research Center's Forum on Religion and Public Life, "2014 U.S. Religious Landscape Survey," www.pewforum.org, Accessed June 16, 2016.

[6] Pew Research Center's Forum on Religion and Public Life, "A Religious Portrait of African Americans," Jan. 30, 2009, www.pewforum.org, Accessed June 24, 2016.

[7] Adelle M. Banks, "Black churches bucking the trend of decline," August 13, 2015, Religion News Service, www.religionnews.com, Accessed June 16, 2016.

[8] Adelle M.Banks, 2015.

[9] Orlando Rodriguez, "2 Sizzling Hot Tech Stocks: NetSuite Inc. (N), CoreLogic, Inc. (CLGX)," August 25, 2016, *The Independent Republic*, www.theindependentrepublic.com, Accessed Sept. 6, 2016.

[10] "Lender discrimination may be pushing black churches into bankruptcy," December 24, 2015, *Chicago Tribune*, www.chicagotribune.com, Accessed September 28, 2016.

[11] Tim Reid, "Banks foreclosing on churches in record numbers," March 9, 2012, Reuters, www.reuters.com, Accessed Sept. 6, 2016.

[12] Paul Brinkmann, "Orlando's 100-year-old black church files bankruptcy," September 27, 2016, *Orlando Sentinel*, www.orlandosentinel.com, Accessed September 28, 2016.

[13] Tim Reid, 2012.

[14] *Powernomics*, p. 239.

[15] Akilah Johnson, "Black-owned banks see surge in deposits," September 10, 2016, *Boston Globe*, www.bostonglobe.com, Accessed September 17, 2016.

[16] David Love, "2016 Nielsen Report: Black Buying Power Has Reached Tipping Point, But How Will Black America Leverage it to Create

Wealth?," *Atlantic Black Star*, February 4, 2016, www.atlanticblackstar.com, Accessed June 15, 2016.

[17] Lou Carlozo, "Black Americans donate to make a difference," Feb. 23, 2012, Reuters, www.reuters.com, Accessed June 20, 2016.

[18] "The Buying Power of Black America – 2010," Target Market News, www.targetmarketnews.com, Accessed June 22, 2016.

[19] "The Black Church: A Brief History," African American Registry, www.aaregistry.org, Accessed June 26, 2016.

[20] Aaron Elstein, "Rev. Calvin Butts seeks salvation for the church-based organization that resurrected Harlem," November 22, 2015, *Crain's New York Business*, www.crainsnewyork.com, Accessed June 27, 2016.

[21] "Economic Stagnation of the Black Middle Class," November 2005, U.S. Commission on Civil Rights, www.usccr.gov, Accessed June 30, 2016.

[22] "African-American middle class," Wikipedia, www.wikipedia.org, Accessed June 30, 2016.

[23] "Black flight," Wikipedia, www.wikipedia.org, Accessed July 1, 2016.

[24] Judy Keen, "Blacks' exodus reshapes cities," May 19, 2011, *USA Today*, www.usatoday.com, Accessed June 30, 2016.

[25] Judy Keen, 2011.

[26] Judy Keen, 2011.

[27] "Black flight," 2016.

[28] Judy Keen, 2011.

[29] "Minority Ownership in Broadcast Stations and Network," National Telecommunications & Information Administration, www.ntia.doc.gov, Accessed July 4, 2016.

[30] Steven G. Vegh, "Influential Hampton Roads Bishop Levi E. Willis Sr. dies," February 20, 2009, *The Virginian-Pilot*, www.pilotonline.com, Accessed July 4, 2016.

[31] NTIA.

[32] Cindy Clayton, "Longtime Newport News Bishop Samuel L. Green Jr. dies at 89," June 29, 2016, *The Virginian-Pilot*, www.pilotonline.com, Accessed July 6, 2016.

[33] Jeanne Lee, "Black-Owned Banks Continue to Feel the Pain of the Recession," February 19, 2016, *The Oklahoman*, www.newsok.com, Accessed June 22, 2016.

[34] Charles Gerena, "Opening the Vault," Spring 2007, *Region Focus*, Federal Reserve Bank of Richmond, www.richmondfed.org, Accessed June 22, 2016.

[35] Charles Gerena, 2007.

[36] Aaron Elstein, "Saving Carver Federal, New York's last black bank,"

March 22, 2015, Crain's New York Business, www.crainsnewyork.com, Accessed June 26, 2016.

[37] Charles Gerena, 2007.

[38] "I've Been to the Mountaintop," Speech delivered by Dr. Martin Luther King Jr. on April 3, 1968 at the Mason Temple, Memphis, Tenn., www.americanrhetoric.com, Accessed June 29, 2016.

[39] Charles Gerena, 2007.

[40] Michael Schwartz, "Bank's heritage consolidated into the history books," September 2, 2010, Richmond Biz Sense, www.richmondbizsense.com, Accessed July 22, 2016.

[41] The Oklahoman, 2016.

[42] Tanasia Kenney, "Ghanaian Company Invests $9M in Failing Black Chicago Bank, Urges Africans and African-Americans to Help One Another," June 29, 2016, Atlanta Black Star, www.atlantablackstar.com, Accessed June 30, 2016.

[43] "African American Banks Reduced to 21—North Milwaukee State Bank Closes," May 5, 2016, HBCU Money, www.hbcumoney.com, Accessed July 25, 2016.

[44] Carolyn M. Brown, "#BankBlack Movement Is Making a Difference in Black Communities," September 17, 2016, Black Enterprise, www.blackenterprise.com, Accessed September 24, 2016.

[45] Akilah Johnson, 2016.

[46] E. Scott Reckard, "Two L.A. Asian American banks near top of national stock ratings," April 22, 2014, Los Angeles Times, www.latimes.com, Accessed September 28, 2016.

[47] "The Difference Between Credit Unions and Banks," Public Service Credit Union, www.pscu.org, Accessed July 16, 2016.

[48] Public Service Credit Union.

[49] Information partially compiled and verified via Credit Union Access, www.creditunionaccess.com, Accessed July 17, 2016.

[50] Jodi Beggs, "What Do Banks Do With Your Money Anyway? Jon Stewart Almost Gets It Right...," April 29, 2010, www.economistsdoitwithmodels.com, Accessed June 25, 2016.

[51] Jodi Beggs, 2010.

[52] Aaron Elstein, Crain's New York Business, March 22, 2015.

[53] Rachel L. Swarns, "Biased Lending Evolves, and Blacks Face Trouble Getting Mortgages," Oct. 30, 2015, The New York Times, Accessed June 26, 2015.

[54] Rachel L. Swarns, 2015.

[55] Rachel L. Swarns, 2015.

[56] Zacks Equity Research, "BancorpSouth Agrees to Settle Suit on Unfair Lending Actions," June 30, 2016, Zacks, www.zacks.com, Accessed July 6, 2016.

[57] Chris Sanchez, "Why Wells Fargo keeps getting into trouble," September 11, 2016, *Business Insider*, www.businessinsider.com, Accessed September 28, 2016.

[58] *PowerNomics*, p. 229.

[59] Darren Thompson and Richard Koon, "A point-by-point guide to comparing loan offers," August 8, 2016, *Church Executive*, www.churchexecutive.com, Accessed September 28, 2016.

[60] Listing for Nannie Helen Burroughs, Wikipedia, www.wikipedia.org, Accessed September 11, 2016.

[61] Gregory Lewis, "Black Bible Scholar Raises Race Questions," February 19, 2006, *Orlando Sun-Sentinel*, www.sun-sentinel.com, Accessed October 6, 2016.

[62] "State of the Bible 2016," American Bible Society, www.americanbible.org, Accessed October 6, 2016.

[63] Luisa Beltran, "Viacom pays $2.3B for BET," November 3, 2000, CNNMoney,www.money.cnn.com, Accessed July 27, 2016.

[64] *Our Black Year: One Family's Quest to Buy Black in America's Racially Divided Economy*, Maggie Anderson, PublicAffairs, 2012, p. xix.

[65] *Our Black Year*, 2012.

[66] *Our Black Year*, 2012.

[67] *Our Black Year*, 2012.

[68] *Our Black Year*, 2012.

[69] *Our Black Year*, 2012.

[70] Steve Daniels, "Pastor-run Covenant Bank fails," February 15, 2013, Crain's Chicago Business, www.chicagobusiness.com, Accessed August 21, 2016.

[71] Bill Winston Ministries website, www.billwinston.com, Accessed August 22, 2016.

[72] *Our Black Year*, p. 229, 2012.

[73] *Our Black Year*, p. 64, 2012.

[74] *Our Black Year*, p. 118, 2012.

[75] *Our Black Year*, p. 136, 2012.

[76] Adelle M. Banks, 2015.

[77] Sandra L. Barnes, *Black Church Giving: An Analysis of Ideological, Programmatic, and Denominational Effects*, June 12, 2013, SAGE Open, www.sgo.sagepub.com, Accessed June 20, 2016.

[78] "Black-Owned Banks Fight to Bounce Back," Jeanne Lee, February 19,

2016, NerdWallet, www.nerdwallet.com, Accessed September 2, 2016.

[79] Jeanne Lee, February 19, 2016.

[80] Akilah Johnson, 2016.

[81] Akilah Johnson, 2016.

[82][82] "$2.1 Million in Scholarships Awarded at the Alfred Street Baptist Church Sponsored HBCU College Festival on Saturday, February 20," February 24, 2016, BlackNews.com, www.blacknews.com, Accessed Sept. 8, 2016.

[83] *Our Black Year*, p.77, 2012.

[84] Christina Montford, "6 Interesting Things You Didn't Know About 'Black Wall Street'," December 2, 2014, *Atlanta Black Star*, www.atlantablackstar.com, Accessed September 30, 2016.

[85] "Friendship-West Launches West Wall Street Movement," April 12, 2016, *Dallas Weekly*, www.dallasweekly.com, Accessed September 22, 2016.

[86] Melissa Kimble, "'Black Wall Street' Being Brought to Life by John Legend and Tika Sumpter," August 23, 2016, *Ebony*, www.ebony.com, Accessed September 22, 2016.

[87] *Dallas Weekly*, 2016.

[88] "38 Black Owned Banks and Credit Unions: Putting Your Money Where It Counts," July 9, 2016, Watch the Yard: Black Greekdom's Digital Yardshow, www.watchtheyard.com, Accessed July 13, 2016.

[89] Garfield Hylton, "Killer Mike Reportedly Has Inspired People To Move Over $800K to Citizens Trust Bank In Only Five Days," July 14, 2016, Uproxx, www.uproxx.com, Accessed July 15, 2016.

[90] Hylton, 2016.

[91] Ann Brown, 2016.

[92] "Cop killings of black men spur $1.25 million in new accounts at Mechanics & Farmers Bank in NC," July 15, 2016, Newsroom Buzz, www.newsroombuzz.com, Accessed July 18, 2016.

[93] Terrell Brown, "Black-Owned Banks See Surge of Applicants Following Protests Against Police Brutality," July 22, 2016, ABC 7 News, www.abc7chicago.com, Accessed July 25, 2016.

[94] John Reosti, "Deposits Surge at Black-Owned Banks After Celeb Appeals," July 20, 2016, *American Banker*, www.americanbanker.com, Accessed July 25, 2016.

[95] Carolyn M. Brown, 2016.

[96] Nathan Bomey, "Black-owned banks get rush of new depositors," July 15, 2016, *USA Today*, www.usatoday.com, Accessed July 16, 2016.

[97] Robert Stitt, "Rappers In Houston Flood Black-Owned Bank to Open

Accounts," July 22, 2016, Financial Juneteenth, www.financialjuneteenth.com, Accessed July 25, 2016.

[98] "Why You Should Move Past 'Deciding' If #BankBlack is for You," Kara I. Stevens, August 12, 2016, *Ebony*, www.ebony.com, Accessed August 30, 2016.

[99] *The Race Beat*, Gene Roberts and Hank Klibanoff, Alfred A. Knopf, 2006, p. 109.

[100] *The Race Beat*, p. 123, 2012.

[101] *Our Black Year*, p. 57, 2012.

[102] *Our Black Year*, p. 137, 2012.

[103] Akilah Johnson, 2016.

Made in the USA
Columbia, SC
21 October 2017